Taking Back Our Classrooms

A Teacher's Perspective
On
America's
Dysfunctional
Education System

Barbara Wood

ISBN: 0692445854
ISBN-15:9780692445853

DEDICATED TO:

Douglas Tureck
&
Norman Rose

CONTENTS

Introduction

Leaving My Country Behind

"Venturing into the Unknown"

9-14

Chapter One

No Challenge Left Behind

"The Lay of the Land"

15-21

Chapter Two

No Country Left Behind

"A Fear-y Tale"

22-32

Chapter Three

No Citizen Left Behind

"Contemplating Our Navels"

33-44

Chapter Four

No Cellphone Left Behind

"Techno-Toiletries Run Rampant"

45-58

Chapter Five

No Censorship Left Behind

"See No Evil, Hear No Evil, Speak No Evil"

59-72

Chapter Six

No Child Left Behind

"Policy Plumbers to the Rescue"

73-93

Chapter Seven

No Corporation Left Behind

"The Customer is Always Right"

94-122

Chapter Eight

No Conversation Left Behind

"Chalk Talk"

123-136

Chapter Nine

No Creativity Left Behind

"Putting the FUN Back into DysFUNction"

137-146

Conclusion

Leaving My Classroom Behind

"A Teary Tale"

147-150

Notes & Bibliography

152-173

Education is not the filling of a pail, but the igniting of a fire.
                                                    -William Butler Yeats

Introduction
Leaving My Country Behind
"Venturing into the Unknown"

I was born into "My country 'tis of thee, sweet land of liberty, of thee I sing." There was a promise contained in being an American. Anything is possible. One can become whatever one wants to become. One is part of the greatest country in the world— a country rooted in democracy with freedoms, opportunities, comforts, and luxuries that not many people in the rest of the world could possibly imagine.

I would get teary-eyed whenever the "Star Spangled Banner" was played, knowing that I was part of a society whose foundation was created by such awe-inspiring, respected forefathers as George Washington, Thomas Jefferson, Benjamin Franklin, and James Madison. Maybe these feelings were all part of being young and idealistic. Nevertheless, they were a part of me.

I grew up in Rye, Colorado. I reveled in the beauty of the countryside in Colorado—the majesty of the mountains, the warmth of the summer sun and crispness of the winter air, the wonder of the four seasons and solace at being part of such magnificence. I went to high school and college in Pueblo, Colorado and always thought I wanted to be a fashion designer or an interior decorator. However, my high school English teacher changed that. Mr. Tureck had a vibrancy for life, for the world around him, and for teaching English. He invited students to embrace the magic of life and all it had to offer. We discussed philosophy, literature, art, music, drama, poetry, and politics, and he encouraged us to think for ourselves. My own aliveness and sense of creativity were awakened. I decided that I, too, wanted to be an English teacher. I, too, wanted to awaken students to the great mysteries and ideas abounding in life and to get them to think for themselves.

I taught for one year at a junior high school in Colorado. However, Australia was hiring American teachers. I had traveled to Mexico and Europe during college, and the travel bug had taken hold. Moreover, my father had been on R and R in Australia during World War II, and he encouraged me to apply to teach there. I accepted a two-year contract in Melbourne and set off on the adventure of my life. With my American pioneer spirit in tow, an abundance of enthusiasm, idealism, and promise for my future as a teacher, I boarded a plane for Australia.

I was like a kid in a candy shop. I was so proud to be a teacher, and I was thrilled that I would be teaching Junior and Senior English, which were university preparatory classes. I would have the chance to teach Camus' *The Stranger*, D.H. Lawrence's *Sons and Lovers*, and Becket's *Waiting for Godot*. What a way to begin a career as an English teacher!

What would become most important to me, however, was my connection with my students. I always wanted to have a down-to-earth, honest, and mutual relationship with them, with humor and laughter added in. Once during a production rehearsal, a student named Justin was supposed to come on stage but didn't appear. Annoyed, I exclaimed, "Where the heck is Justin? He just missed his cue." His head popped around from behind my chair; he laughed, "I'm right behind you, Miss Wood. I'm painting 'DIRECTOR' on the back of your chair!" Annoyance dissolved into laughter.

My rapport with students is what anchored me to the profession. When they wrote me letters thanking me for what they felt I had given them, or when they unexpectedly came to visit me at school or at home, even years after they had graduated, I knew that I had chosen a meaningful and rewarding profession.

As the years progressed, I not only taught English but drama/theatre, speech, media studies, alternative lifestyles, and even Australian history. But, what always held steady was my rapport with students. Schools there had a relaxed atmosphere. Parents and students accepted teachers' differences, making for colorful school environments, and they respected teachers' expertise. Still, twenty-six years later, the "wild, wild West," the mountains of Colorado, and my family beckoned me, even though I had a meaningful job and a wonderful network of Australian friends.

In August, 2002, I boarded a plane with a one-way ticket back to the land of my origin and a job in a small town in Colorado. I was looking forward to teaching in the U.S. During the twenty-four hour plane journey I drifted into a disturbed sleep. I dreamed I was on a space craft rocketing into outer space—into the great beyond—into the mysterious universe. I traveled for about a week and then jetted back to earth to find that twenty-six years had lapsed. Everything on earth had changed.

When I told a friend about the dream, she laughed, "Duh, Barbara. Think about it. It makes sense. You've been living in Australia for twenty-six years, and now you have returned to the U.S. where things have most certainly changed." Those changes were what I would be grappling with for the next thirteen years.

Gas-guzzling trucks and SUV's twice the size of average vehicles hogged the streets, creating traffic hazards for drivers of compact cars who couldn't see over or around them. Hazards especially for someone like me who was learning to re-negotiate driving on the right side of the road.

Obese people everywhere! Apples, oranges, peaches, potatoes, and zucchini had doubled in size but not in flavor. Plates in restaurants heaped with fried foods—"culinary delights" smothered in cheese, sauces, and sour cream—more for the money but to the detriment of your health.

Television ads hawked every over-the-counter drug imaginable—drugs for allergies, asthma, colds, diabetes, osteoporosis, hemorrhoids, cholesterol, pain relief, weight loss, insomnia, hair growth, erectile dysfunction, and stomach relief (for gas, constipation, and diarrhea resulting from eating restaurant and junk food, no doubt).

Polarized politics split the country between Democrats and Republicans; between the blue states and the red states. In Congress neither side would concede an inch to the other. Politicians and public figures were forced to apologize for opinions or comments that offended individuals or groups. Political correctness ran rampant, wielded as a weapon to pin down and undermine opponents. Radical radio and TV commentators bated the public.

The most unsettling differences related to education. No Child Left Behind and state-mandated testing were two concepts that framed American education policy of the twenty-first century. Other over-prescriptive policies plagued the system: children's rights, child abuse, sexual harassment, bullying, and school safety, to name a few. Each of these policies framed—stifled—relationships between teachers, students, parents, and administrators because they were spelled out in minute detail in terms of "appropriate" and "inappropriate" behavior expectations. Not that I didn't believe these issues were important, but that the policies that framed them had become too prescriptive and stifling, not allowing much leverage for spontaneous interactions among individuals.

Entitled students and entitled, helicopter parents demanded their rights. A band teacher was called into the counseling office to be told that several students complained that she didn't smile enough in class. A student had filed a report with a Dean of Students, complaining that she didn't like the way another student looked at her in class. A mother complained to an art teacher for the "B" her daughter got in art because the mother "knew" that her daughter was a "talented 'A' student." Another mother told a French teacher that she wasn't going to listen to what the teacher told her about her daughter because she knew it wasn't true. The teacher had tried to explain that the reason her daughter had a "D" in French was because she hadn't done her homework and had failed to submit several assignments. The mother had the counselor remove her daughter from class, even though it was only a month before the end of the year-long class.

A student threatened a teacher with her father's profession as a litigation lawyer when the teacher refused to give her points to boost her grade. A student snapped at me, threatening that she could sue me when I placed a hand on her shoulder in encouragement. Some students demanded that I boost their grades by giving them extra points they hadn't earned. An angry parent abused me in an email for the role her son got in a musical, accusing me of purposely giving him a role he didn't want.

Since I had maintained a friendship with the English teacher who had inspired me to become a teacher, I told him how disconcerting I found the attitudes of students and parents. Never in twenty-six years of teaching in Australia had students and parents spoken to me in the way that they did here in the United States. He related how he could have taught forever—his passion was that great—but in the early 90s he began to observe that when issues arose with students and parents, school administrators indulged the students and parents—to the disregard of their teachers. Administrators had become de facto culprits because they allowed the students and parents to run schools. He could see what was ahead for teachers and decided to retire—a dedicated and gifted teacher lost to the system.

I had heard of the *boiling frog* myth which states that if a frog is dropped into a pot of boiling water it will feel the heat and jump out of the pot. But if you put the frog in a pot of tepid water and turn the heat on low, it will sit there placidly and sink into a stupor as the water gradually heats up, unaware of the danger it is in. It will unresistingly boil to death. I was like the frog dropped into the boiling water of education. Because I lived in Australia for so many years and wasn't in the U.S. during the time that the changes I found frustrating had taken place, these changes were possibly affecting me more than they did American teachers who had never experienced any other education system. I felt trapped. I found myself angry at the entitled parents and students, angry at the administrators who indulged them, angry at policies I had no say in and that I felt were psychologically and educationally unsound, and angry at my professional disenfranchisement!

I decided to get my master's degree in adult education. I hoped that I could impact education by working with student teachers, parents, and administrators. I wanted to make them aware of the educational quagmire. Unfortunately, my delving into current research by psychologists, philosophers, sociologists, political scientists, and educators bore out my worst perceptions— that an entitlement mentality; a policy and procedure driven education system based on corporate values; the censorship of ideas within the classroom; and students' pervasive interest in social networking and technology are having debilitating effects on American education.

I then remembered a poignant moment during my first year of teaching. My ninth grade English class was studying *The Diary of Ann Frank*. A German student who had recently become an American citizen, along with his mother, said that his mother had been a child during Hitler's rise to power in Germany. She wanted to talk to the class about her experience. She had gone to a German school where she had been indoctrinated to think that Hitler was Germany's savior. Even most German adults came to believe that he was. Germans starving after WWI were looking to be rescued. Hitler eloquently led them to believe that he could save them. He controlled the school system and the media, telling Germans only what he wanted them to believe. The woman's father even became an SS officer in Hitler's army (he was in the lower ranks of the army); and when he realized what was really going on, he tried to defect but was killed for his disloyalty to Hitler. It wasn't until after the war, however, that the woman and her mother became aware of the atrocities being committed by Hitler. She was haunted by the Nazi deception and said that she would spend the rest of her life trying to understand it.

This woman's anguished testimony had always stayed with me. As I thought about it, I realized that when individuals are conditioned or immersed in a society or culture their perceptions of what is happening around them are often myopic. Outsiders often perceive the situation from a broader perspective because they haven't been "conditioned" in that society or culture. I began to soften my judgments of parents and students. However, my criticism of the system did not abate. I still felt that what was happening to teachers and students was bordering on criminal, and the condition needed to be addressed! The future of American society was in jeopardy if we Americans didn't take a long, hard look at what was happening. Today's students were supposed to be being prepared as tomorrow's citizens and leaders.

As a teacher, I want to share my thoughts and perspectives on what's needed to establish and maintain a worthwhile public education system. This book is my contribution to the public dialogue.

Chapter One
No Challenge Left Behind
"The Lay of the Land"

In her June, 2010 valedictory address, Erica Goldson from Coxsackie-Athens High School in New York stated:

> We are so focused on a goal, whether it be passing
> a test, or graduating first in the class. However,
> in this way, we do not really learn. . .perhaps you
> only learned how to memorize names, places,
> and dates to later on forget in order to clear
> your mind for the next test. School is not all that
> it can be. Right now, it is a place for most people
> to determine that their goal is to get out as soon
> as possible. . I cannot say that I am any more
> intelligent than my peers. I can attest that I am
> only the best at doing what I am told and working
> the system. . .[1]

Erica's comments speak volumes about her disillusionment with the current education system. In 2005 teacher B. Starnes, feeling incompetent and unsure of herself because of what was happening in education, obtained her doctorate degree in an effort to feel more secure in her job. However, she came to the disillusioned conclusion:

> I misjudged how one becomes an educational expert.
> I thought it had something to do with thought,

experience, deep thinking, reflective practice,
and the study of theory and research. And maybe
there was a time when that was true. But in today's
educational climate, it isn't. . .In the meantime I am
worried about the frightening nightmares I have
begun to have while awake. Education has fallen
into a rabbit hole. The Mad Hatter is making the
rules, the Queen of Hearts keeps pounding on
education with a croquet mallet, and the hurrieder
we get in our educational system, the behinder
we get.[2] (p. 3).

Starnes' comments speak volumes about her frustrations with being a teacher in the current education system.

Teachers and students are floundering to meet the requirements of a policy, procedure, and data-driven education system that expects teachers to follow mandated education policies and standardized curriculum. It's a system that coddles and rescues students in an attempt to "leave no child behind," and fosters conformity rather than true critical thinking and personal responsibility. It is a system that is creating citizens who will rely on being rescued, rather than becoming critically-thinking adults capable of participating responsibly in a democratic society.

American education is at a crossroads. It's time to ask the relevant questions: What is education? Should data drive the system? Does such a system hijack the learning process? Is "corporate education" opposed to learning? Why do students need to be made successful in the same way? Is an entitlement mentality compromising teachers' professionalism in the classroom because parents' and students' demands are often given deference regardless of true benefit to students? Is the escalation of digital technology and social networking having negative effects on students' abilities to learn? Are many of today's youth becoming the distracted generation, immersed in a world of social networking which is diminishing their interest in education? Are censorship issues stunting students' higher level thinking skills?

Learning entails exploration and being allowed to learn from mistakes. At present, the American system has mandated this process out of existence. Government policies such as "No Child

Left Behind" and "Race to the Top" undermine education by establishing unrealistic, unattainable goals.

Blaming teachers for the problems in education is a simplistic solution to a complex situation. "Weeding out" seemingly incompetent teachers won't solve the problems. Besides, who and what determine "incompetence" in the field of personality, character, impact, and knowledge?

We need to take up the challenge and have a realistic look at the issues that are creating problems within America's public education system.

Plan for the Book

In this book I explore American public education from a teacher's perspective. It's become popular to blame teachers for the current dysfunction in the system. But, from a teacher's perspective, there are a number of pertinent issues and circumstances that impinge on our ability to be effective in the classroom. In this book, I hope to make readers aware of these issues. The book is divided into ten chapters whose titles are based on the acronym NCLB (No Child Left Behind). The assertions made in each chapter are supported by examples from my and other teachers' experiences in the classroom. They are then underpinned with extensive research.

- **Introduction, Leaving My Country Behind**, is testimony of my observations and experiences of American society and its education system upon my return to the U.S. after teaching in Australia for twenty-six years. The chapter explains the conflicts I felt about my career upon my return. I began a personal journey to comprehend why I found teaching in the U.S. to be an overwhelmingly negative experience after having loved my career for so long.

- **Chapter Two, No Country Left Behind**, establishes the cultural context for the current education system. The chapter focuses on the litigious, fear-based nature of American society and on how education reform is based on our fear of being left behind as a superpower. I suggest that this fear has been projected onto the education system and underpins our dysfunctional approach to public education.

- **Chapter Three, No Citizen Left Behind**, explores the narcissistic, entitled attitudes of parents and students that are hijacking the education system and paralyzing teachers' professional input into education, and more specifically, within the classroom. The chapter explores the historical context that has led to the U.S. becoming a nation with entitlement attitudes. The psychological ramification of these attitudes, especially within schools, is crippling.

- **Chapter Four, No Cell Phone Left Behind**, investigates how social networking and digital technology may be impacting students' intellectual, emotional, and social development, affecting their ability to learn or to want to learn. The chapter questions whether formal education is becoming irrelevant to many students who are becoming addicted to social networking. Current research is also cited concerning the effects of multi-tasking on the brain and on children's cognitive development. I suggest that it is easier to blame teachers for students' lack of academic success or to mandate more testing and data collection than it is to analyze and deal with the complexity of the situation.

- **Chapter Five, No Censorship Left Behind**, exposes the effects of politically correct and conservative interest groups on public education. These groups have applied pressure on textbook publishers, test-preparation companies, and state education agencies to alter language and actions within textbooks and on tests that might be considered offensive by sub-groups of race, gender, sexual orientation, disability, religion, and political views. In turn, textbook publishers, test-preparation companies, and state education agencies have complied with these demands lest they be sued for noncompliance. In the meantime, teachers are gagged, and students are dumbed down. Further testing and data collection isn't going to alter students' lack of higher level thinking skills.

- **Chapter Six, No Child Left Behind**, explains how unrealistic policies and procedures are driving education. The U.S.'s entitlement mentality and litigious nature, which has led to interest groups pushing for government policies, is being mirrored in schools. Mandated policies regulate every conceivable interaction or situation—imagined or real—within a school. Policies predetermine how individuals will relate to each other in given situations in an attempt to "head off any problems at the pass." The most grievous policy, which is discussed at length in this chapter, is that of No Child Left Behind. Students and teachers are straight-jacketed by a national policy, not of their making, which has wrongly informed public education for the greater part of the twenty-first century.

- **Chapter Seven, No Corporation Left Behind**, reveals that the disturbing trend in schools is their transformation from public institutions, influenced by community collaboration, to that of profit-making, entrepreneurial entities based on free-market ideology. Besides being infiltrated by corporate-based partnerships, schools are being structured along corporate guidelines. "Corporate education" conjures up images of stakeholders, customers, clients, business plans, high-stakes testing, charter schools, vouchers, choice, school-business partnerships, merit pay, accountability, CEO-type management, performance-based outcomes, and product-based education rather than education as a process. Teachers are especially held hostage, unable to exercise their expertise in the classroom, because parents and students wield the power in a "customer is always right" atmosphere. Because, if students decide to "choice out" of a school, the school's funding will be affected. Behind the scenes, education is also being undermined by powerful private foundations and their corporate heads. Well-known entrepreneurs such as Bill Gates, Eli and Edythe Broad, the Walton family (of Walmart fame), and the Koch brothers have established foundations whose sole motives are to reform American education on their terms.

- **Chapter Eight, No Conversation Left Behind**, challenges educators, specifically teachers, and experts in child psychology, learning theory, human behavior, pedagogy, knowledge transfer, and the art of teaching, learning, and curriculum development to participate in a conversation about public education reform. Teachers must be at the helm of this conversation rather than politicians, policy makers, and corporate executives. These individuals need to listen to the true experts and then implement their recommendations. My contribution to the conversation is from the perspective of a teacher who has remained in the classroom for thirty-eight years. From this vantage point, and from the extensive research that I have conducted, I suggest that we learn from other countries such as Finland, get rid of many of the policies that frame the current system, and replace the corporate framework with a philosophical framework that understands the stages of human development and learning.

- **Chapter Nine, No Creativity Left Behind**, expresses the belief that a focus on creativity within public education would have a transformative and healing effect on a dysfunctional system and society. Such a focus would balance the current data-collecting, record-keeping, punitive approach by consciously embracing the creative impulse within all of us. The chapter explains why this focus is crucial and how it would develop autonomy and self-directed learning within our coddled and overly monitored students. The chapter offers practical recommendations on how to implement such a program.

- **Chapter Ten, Leaving My Classroom Behind**, is testimony to my decision to leave behind my career. I reflect on what being a teacher has meant to me and discuss what truly constitutes "being a teacher" from my perspective. I also ponder what the future of public education will be if we don't act now to change direction.

And so, in the following pages, I present my case to you.

Chapter Two
No Country Left Behind
"A Fear-y Tale"

January 28, 1986 was an unforgettable day. It was the day the Challenger Space Shuttle was launched. For the first time ever, an ordinary American citizen—a teacher Christa McAuliffe— would be aboard as part of the crew.

In Australia, I watched the event as it was televised around the world. The rocket left the pad to the murmurs and awe of all who gathered at Nassau. Seventy-three seconds later, the craft disintegrated before the eyes of the world. Had someone set off fireworks in celebration? The camera panned the watching crowd, narrowing in on the faces of Christa's parents and family. Frozen looks of disbelief.

I felt anxiety as tears trickled down my face. A feeling of helplessness about life and its uncertainties took hold. I could imagine how Christa's family must have felt in those moments. How shocked they must have been at losing Christa in a flash of light and not being able to do anything about it, not being able to control the situation or rescue her from her fate.

As I reflected on the fear and uncertainty created by the Challenger disaster, I saw a parallel in twenty-first century American society and its education system. It seems to me that the U.S. is experiencing the same type of fear and uncertainty concerning its superpower status— and those attitudes are being projected onto our education system. The nature of this fear, plus our "fear of the enemy," must be explored before other issues within education can be addressed. These other issues emanate from this fear.

Novelists, philosophers, psychologists, and sociologists have written about how deep-seated primal fears and existential angst compel us to act in the ways we do. *Why are we here? What does it mean to be human? Is there a God? Am I in control of my own destiny? Are there any certainties in life other than death?*

Herman Melville's *Moby Dick* grappled with such questions. Ahab is obsessed with the primal need to control his life and his destiny. His leg, ripped off in an encounter at sea with the great white whale Moby Dick, drives him to avenge its loss by ruthlessly pursuing and killing Moby Dick, whom he sees as the embodiment of evil. Ahab and his crew are tossed to and fro at sea by the furious, merciless brute whale. Even so, Ahab is equally unrelenting, which leads to the final sinking of his ship. Ahab's "inner journey" culminates in his raising his fist towards the heavens and crying out in anguish, *"Is it I, God, or who that lifts this arm?"* The uncertainty of life is more than he can bear, and it is his quest to conquer uncertainty that leads to his demise.[1]

In his short story "To Build a Fire," Jack London shows us a man who is the opposite of Ahab. He is oblivious of primal doubts and uncertainties. Journeying across the Yukon in fifty-degrees-below-zero weather, the man is intent upon meeting friends at an old claim by six o'clock that night. London tells us that the man is alert to the "things" in life but not to the "significances." Fifty-degrees-below-zero is merely fifty-degrees-below-zero. Because of his inability to discern the perilous situation he is in and the conditions in life that are beyond his control, the man freezes to death in the snow. The dog, who cannot understand why the man "sleeps" when he should be building a fire to keep warm, sniffs death and runs in the direction of "the food-providers and the fire-providers" further down the trail.[2]

The men in these stories dealt with the uncertainties of life in different ways, illustrating the unique makeup of each character. These different responses are what make humankind so complex and varied.

The premise of Ernest Becker's Pulitzer-Prize-winning psych-philosophical book *The Denial of Death* is that we feel helpless and abandoned in a terrifying world that we cannot fully comprehend. We are given life and yet we are fated to die. Thus, the basic motive for human behavior stems from a need to control this primal anxiety.

Because the terror is so overwhelming, we bury it deep within our psyches, creating defense mechanisms to protect us from feelings of helplessness and uncertainty. Becker theorized that we live within cultures, societies, and nations that allow us to establish group identities which make us feel safe.[3] In fact, my experience living in Australia for twenty-six years taught me that nations and societies, composed of different cultures and belief systems, also have different ways of dealing with primal doubts.

Becker observed that nations often aim to destroy what they perceive to be evil in the world to make themselves feel more secure in their beliefs. Thus, quests to do so equate to "my God against your God," my belief system against your belief system, the values within my culture against the values within your culture. "We want to clean up the world, make it perfect, keep it safe for democracy or communism, purify it of the enemies of God, and eliminate evil."[4] And, ironically, all we ultimately do is create more strife, uncertainty, and insecurity in the world.

Joseph Campbell, renowned mythologist, writer, and lecturer, developed theories about cultural development that are relevant to Becker's ideas. Stepping out of the "western paradigm," Campbell gained an objective understanding about how cultures, societies, and nations create "myths," or invented stories, that become the foundations upon which they operate and give meaning to life. Having studied cultures around the world, both past and present, Campbell concluded that humans need these stories to create a sense of belonging and security.[5]

Becker's and Campbell's ideas are relevant to American society. The American story began when our forefathers penned the "Declaration of Independence" which held "certain truths to be self-evident that all men are created equal, that they are endowed by their Creator with certain inalienable Rights, among these are Life, Liberty, and the Pursuit of Happiness."[6] America was a country with wide-open spaces, often referred to as the "last frontier," an expansive country with unlimited opportunity for all. Individuals could create the lives they so desired. And, as happens when any new society comes into being, the dawning of America entailed subjugating the stories of other native cultures.

The American pioneer spirit that settled this country was such that individuals had to embrace the uncertainties in life. O. E.

Rolvaag's novel *Giants in the Earth* portrays many of the uncertainties that Norwegian immigrants to the U.S. had to face: harsh winters, failed crops, fear of being attacked by unfriendly Indians, living isolated in the wilderness, running out of supplies, a yearning to return to the homeland. However, the pioneer spirit prevailed and became part of the early American story.[7]

As American society evolved so did the idea of the "American Dream," a phrase coined by James Adams in his book *The Epic of America* written in 1931. The story was still of a land where everyone could have a better, richer, and fuller life based on an individual's innate capabilities or achievements.[8]

However, American society no longer fits the story given birth so many years ago. That story allowed individuals to grapple with their own personal experiences of uncertainty within the framework of a democratic society. Today, we have a policy-driven society. It's as if we think that by over-developing policies that regulate human behavior we will eradicate uncertainty from the human experience. As Philip K. Howard states in his book *The Death of Common Sense*:

> The law of government. . .controls almost every
> activity of common interest—fixing the potholes
> in front of the house, running public schools,
> regulating day care centers, controlling behavior in
> the workplace. . . and deciding whether Mother
> Teresa gets a building permit.[9] (p. 5).

That isn't to say that we don't need any rules, regulations, policies, or laws, because we do, but it seems that the pendulum has swung to over-regulating human behavior, and we now need to seek a balance.

Since the 1960s, our nation has passed law after law intended to ensure the rights of various interest groups such as children, women, the elderly, the disabled, the mentally challenged, and racial minorities, to name a few. While such concerns are noble in nature, as more and more groups demand their rights, different groups' rights are likely to infringe on the rights of other groups.

Adhering to all the laws and respecting the rights of others can be a daunting task. The system does not allow for mistakes because "being human" has been legislated out of existence. Rather, we somehow believe that if we create enough laws we can obliterate uncertainty from life and create perfect citizens. In fact, such an approach creates more uncertainty. People become anxiety-ridden lest they make mistakes. Also, because uncertainty is a natural phenomenon, it needs to be accepted as such. Legislating uncertainty out of existence can create neurotic individuals who live straitjacketed, homogenized, repressed lives. Any number of anti-social behaviors can surface when people feel repressed.

Heaven help us if we ever evolve to the state illustrated in the sci-fi movie *Minority Report*. Set in the year 2054, a specialized police department called "Pre-crime" apprehends criminals before they have committed crimes based on foreknowledge provided by psychics called "precogs." With the technology that is increasingly available to us, science fiction could become science fact.[10]

Living in a legalistic society has created a litigious mentality. Those fixated on rules, regulations, and policies tend to sue others who don't follow these rules, regulations, and policies. Thus, we have created a blame culture of individuals "who know their rights" and will go to any lengths to insure that they get them or will sue others who infringe on them. One example of the effect that a litigious mentality has had on the work world is that of employers giving references for employees. It has become common practice among some public and private entities to refuse to provide references for former employees. Providing references is considered too risky because the business or agency could either be sued by former employees for giving unfavorable references or sued by prospective employers for giving good references when the new employee didn't measure up.

Thus, the land of freedom has become entrenched in a legal maze of mandated rules, regulations, and procedures.[11] The land founded on the declaration that "all men are created equal" and on the belief that in a land of opportunity each person's unique abilities will determine their achievements in life has become a land that mandates equality regardless of ability or achievement. In doing so, individuality is erased. If individuals lack in the ability to do something, the system has laws that over-compensate for them so they never have to grapple with their limitations. Many Americans, especially today's youth, never have to face the realities of life or of being human. We are not all the same. We have different abilities, strengths, and weaknesses that make us unique.

Not only is American society concerned with alleviating uncertainty, but true to Becker's observations, it is a society that has been based on "fear of an enemy." After World War II and up until the Soviet Union's collapse in 1991, the enemy was Russia and communism. After 911 the enemy has been the Middle East, Islam, and terrorism. Fear has become intrinsic to the American psyche and culture.

Magical memories stir within me when I recall growing up in the small mountain town of Rye, Colorado in the 1950s and 60s. Our pink cottage, with its picturesque view of Mt. Baldy, was set close to the road that wound up the mountainside. In summer, I spent days roaming the countryside with my dog Blackie at my side and time sitting next to a creek mesmerized by the rush of water as it traveled the creek bed. In autumn, there were hayrides to go on and bonfires to rally around in the evenings. Winter brought days of sledding on our neighbors' hill and Christmas caroling with my church's youth group. During our church's Christmas program, we would hold candles while singing Christmas carols. Santa Claus would burst through the door, giving everyone a brown paper bag filled with Christmas candy. Heading home in the silent night in our two-door, light blue Ford, we would pass "Rattle Snake Hill," which was lit by a giant Christmas star. All was right in the world.

However, behind closed doors at night, in bed, I would often lay awake frightened of a nuclear war because America was fraught with the fear of being invaded by Russia. During the Bay of Pigs and Cuban Missile Crisis, I remember that the talk at the dinner table concerned putting an air raid siren in our backyard since our property was strategically located within the small mountain community. Neighbors and friends discussed building bomb shelters and securing basements as refuges from an attack. I worried about how my entire family of six would cram into the tiny dirt room that was our basement. I also knew that my mother loved her antique heirlooms and furniture, and I wondered how we could quickly move them to the basement before the attack.

Three minutes to midnight. Military Industrial Complex. Armament. Anti-ballistic missiles. Arms Race. Communism. Escalation. Cold War. Communism. Nuclear fallout. First- strike capability. Limited test-ban treaty. Containment. Détente. These concepts and words became part of the American vocabulary.

Years later, I came across a Ron Cobb cartoon that depicted the fear I had felt as a child. A little boy is lying in his bed at night with a terrified look on his face. Looming above his bed, engulfing the room, is a nuclear bomb. The caption for the cartoon reads "Child Abuse."[12]

As I grew older and paid more attention to the news and took political science classes in college, I began to wonder if Russia really was a threat or if the U.S. needed an enemy to rail against for political reasons that were too complicated for the average American to comprehend. However, whether the threat was real or not, American society was becoming fear-based—not the sort of adrenalin-rush fear experienced when stepping on a rattlesnake or hearing someone break into your house, but a more insidious, systemic fear that settles into people's psyches, becoming an unconscious part of their being—similar to breathing, eating, and sleeping. So, not only are many Americans frightened of the uncertainties of life, they also have an ingrained fear of "the enemy."

My perception of America being a fear-based society became more obvious after I lived in Australia for twenty-six years, from 1976 to 2002, and experienced a society, at that particular point in time, that didn't foster the fear of an enemy that must be fought and defeated. Although Australian society went through its "Yellow Peril" phase (fear of Japanese/Asian invasion after World War II), most of this fear dissipated in the 1970s, unlike that in the United States.

Then came September 11, 2001. I was lying in bed in my cabin in the Australian bush when the phone rang. A friend called to say that she just heard on the radio that New York City had been attacked! All I could think of was King Kong climbing up the Empire State Building. The continental U.S. had never been attacked before, so what was going on? I turned on the TV to see repeated footage of a plane plowing into the Twin Towers.

Pandemonium in the streets, clouds of thick grey dust everywhere. People running. People confused. Sounds of sirens. The toppling of both towers. A plane plows into the Pentagon while another one crashes in a field in Pennsylvania. Terrorist acts on a grand scale. The chaos. The fear. The pain. The grief. The vulnerability of a nation that had been seemingly invincible. These are the scenes viewed on TV, from a distance, happening somewhere else in the world—not in the U.S. The unthinkable had become thinkable; the unimaginable, imaginable.

The U.S., like Ahab, would become obsessed with conquering the enemy. The Patriot Act was passed, and security was stepped up in airports, train and bus stations, and at large public events. Talk of securing borders to prevent access by illegal aliens commenced. The daily news informed Americans of the level of the terrorist threat for each day. The "land of the free and home of the brave" was being held hostage. A country that prided itself on its democracy and freedom was developing an "at siege" mentality that would permeate all aspects of society.

Within this context, President Bush instituted the No Child Left Behind policy, which would frame national education policy for the next decade and possibly beyond. A policy mirroring a society riddled with fear and uncertainty, it would focus on the fear of children being "left behind" within the American education system. This policy would attempt to socially engineer a "psychologically correct" education system based on the assumption that every child can make the academic grade and reach established academic benchmarks. Factors such as lack of student motivation, limited ability, social disadvantages, poverty, and limited or inequitable distribution of education funding across the nation would not inform the policy. No Child Left Behind would put unrealistic expectations and goals on educators and students.

To "leave behind" or to "be left behind" is part of the human condition, equating to change, growth, and evolution. Leaving behind a mother's womb, growing older, and eventually dying are inevitable transitions. Choosing to leave home, to move to a different place, to end a relationship, or to find a new job are choice transitions. In either case, one must deal with the feelings involved with these transitions, as must those individuals who are "left behind" because of other people's decisions. Feelings such as fear, disappointment, uncertainty, regret, excitement, and anticipation once dealt with can lead to personal growth.

However, implementation of NCLB stunts the personal growth of our youth because they are not allowed to experience a fundamental aspect of being human—that of learning to cope. I doubt President Bush understood that he would be tampering with a natural law of life when he mandated such a policy and that he was setting the youth of our country on a path of "arrested development" because educators would have to resort to rescue tactics rather than learning strategies in order to meet the stringent, unrealistic, and punitive mandates of the policy.

Perhaps, what is of more concern than this attempt at creating a "psychologically correct" education system is the fact that presidents, politicians, and policymakers may have a hidden agenda that has nothing to do with the welfare of our youth but has everything to do with the threat of losing our superpower status. The United States has reveled in global super-powerdom since World War II, and this status has defined us. Our dominance has been in military, economic, political, intellectual, and cultural realms. However, in recent years there have been indications that U.S. global influence is declining. According to Robert Pape of "The National Interest" magazine:

> The self-inflicted wounds of the Iraq war, growing government debt, increasingly negative current-accounts balances, and other economic weaknesses have cost the United States real power in today's world. . .if present trends continue we will look back at the Bush administration's years as the death knell of American hegemony.[13] (p. 21).

In July 2011, PEW Global Attitudes Project conducted a survey and found that fifteen of twenty-two nations surveyed expressed doubts about America's superpower status. The balance of opinion is that China either will replace or already has replaced the U.S. as the world's leading superpower. This view is especially widespread in Western Europe where at least six in ten people in France (72%), Spain (67%), Britain (65%), and Germany (61%) see China overtaking the U.S.[14]

Could it indeed be that our leaders are more concerned about the U.S. being "left behind" than about our children being "left behind?" Could it be that, out of fear of losing superpower status, a desperate attempt is being made to make American youth look good at all costs education-wise in order to maintain our number one status in the world, especially in the education realm where we seem to lag behind other nations?

Results from a 2012 international test administered by the Program for International Student Assessment (PISA) showed that the performance of American students who took the tests differed little from the performance of those tested in 2009. In fact, the U.S. has demonstrated no significant improvement on these international tests since 2003, despite all the national testing and data collecting which is the U.S.'s current "reform" strategy. The PISA results showed that, as in previous years, top rankings in math, science, and reading were from students in Shanghai, Hong Kong, Singapore, Japan, and South Korea. American fifteen-year-olds scored in the middle of developed countries in reading and science and lagged in math. In math, twenty-nine countries had higher test scores than the U.S., while in science twenty-two countries did better, and in reading, nineteen countries. The percentage of students who scored at the highest levels in math and science was much greater in several Asian and European countries. The most disturbing fact is that American students do poorly when it comes to creative thinking and problem solving when it comes to applying math concepts to real life problems.[15]

Fearing the long-term repercussions of such education performance on the future economic viability of the country, the Obama Administration's education policy, "Race to the Top," has continued the push for comprehensive education reform during his time in office.

The approach U.S. leaders and policy-makers are taking in education reform is dysfunctional—similar to that of over-solicitous parents who are frightened of losing control and influence over their children lest they become something other than what the parents want them to become. Such an approach doesn't allow children to develop their own personalities, make their own mistakes, carve their own destinies, or establish a level of autonomy.

In effect, such an approach is anathema in a country that prides itself on being a republic that upholds freedom, individualism, and autonomy as its basic tenants. These tenants require citizens who are critical, creative thinkers who can take responsibility for their own thoughts and actions.

Teaching in Australia during the period of time that I did, allowed me to be part of a society that wasn't obsessed with remaining the world's single superpower with all of its ego trappings. While it was important for educators to strive to help students do their best, there was not an urgency to make every student achieve the same ends. It was accepted that students had differing abilities and differing strengths and weaknesses, which did not make them failures if they were unable to achieve rigidly established benchmarks. And, teachers certainly weren't targeted or blamed for students' lack of achievement. Ironically, Australia is ranked ahead of the U.S. in reading, math, and science in the OECD performance results.

Nations such as Finland and South Korea are top scorers on the Program for International Assessment. They have eliminated the crowded testing schedules used decades ago when these nations were ranked much lower. By contrast, the Obama administration, backed by corporate foundations, is intensifying testing at all levels—viewing such measures as innovative "reform" rather than what it actually has always been: insanity.[16]

The recent documentary "The Finland Phenomenon" explores Finland's highly successful education system. Finland excels in the world in innovation, entrepreneurship, and creativity. The Finnish government rejects testing as a means for getting students to do well in school, and it promotes teaching as a highly esteemed profession. The government believes in nurturing its teachers rather than denigrating them. Also, the tax and social welfare systems ensure that education quality doesn't vary across class lines as it does in the U.S.[17]

Why does education have to be a "race to the top?" We need to look to countries whose education systems are different from ours and whose students are thriving. What is it that they are doing differently? Does fear drive their education systems? Are they primarily concerned with carving out or maintaining political and economic power and status in the world, or do they have a genuine concern in educating their youth for a posterity that has not only economic but intrinsic value for all concerned?

Chapter Three
No Citizen Left Behind
"Contemplating Our Navels"

Peter and Wendy, children in Ray Bradbury's 1951 short story "The Veldt," are nothing like the children in "Peter Pan." Peter and Wendy in "Peter Pan" represent childhood innocence seeking fantasy. Bradbury's children are emotionally detached, spoiled, and manipulative victims of over-indulgent parents and a technological, consumer society. They live in a sound-proofed Happy-Life Home that clothes and feeds them, rocks them to sleep, and plays and sings to them. In their specially designed nursery, all they have to do is think thoughts, and the room telepathically transforms into whatever they imagine or desire. The assumption is that children will think only happy, innocent thoughts.[1]

When Peter and Wendy begin transforming the nursery into an African veldt where lions kill their prey, their parents decide to turn off the nursery and the house so they all can begin to live "authentic" lives. Throwing tantrums, the children convince their parents to give them one more night in the nursery. They lure their parents into the room, which has "come alive." The lions await their prey. Peter and Wendy are left to live self-centered, indulgent lives forevermore.[2]

When he penned this science fiction story in 1951, did Bradbury know he was forecasting the future? Narcissism—excessive love or admiration of oneself—can develop when individuals are overindulged and feel a sense of entitlement. A number of books and scholarly articles document what is happening in American culture: *Culture of Narcissism, The Narcissism Epidemic, American Narcissism: The Myth of National Superiority, Prisoners of Childhood: The Drama of the Gifted*

Child and the Search for the True Self, The Death of Common Sense, and *A Nation of Wimps.*

The first time I noticed this mindset was in 2004 as a teacher in an American classroom. I decided to take seven students on a theater trip to New York City. We had a great time seeing the sights, taking theater workshops, and attending Broadway productions. But, on the day of our departure a blizzard set in, and our plane was grounded. We had to wait until the storm passed to get a flight out of Newark. Because we had to get a connecting flight in St. Paul/Minneapolis to get back to Colorado, we would miss that flight and have to stay overnight in the twin cities.

The airline had managed to reschedule two students on a flight direct from Newark to Denver once the storm was over. When I told the group who would be flying home, pandemonium broke out. The two girls didn't want to fly with each other but wanted to fly with other students. I explained that the airline had determined who would fly out and that I had no control over it. One girl couldn't understand why her friend couldn't just take the other ticket and pretend she was the ticketed passenger. I told her that wasn't feasible because of the strict airline regulations implemented after the 911 attacks.

Then, without my knowing, students got on their cellphones and called their parents complaining about the situation. Over the next hour, I had phone calls from five parents demanding that their child be put on the flight from Newark because of family plans at home. I was bewildered. I couldn't understand why the students and parents could be so demanding. I explained that my decisions would be based on what was decided by the airlines and what was best for the entire group. Dealing with the Newark blizzard was bad enough, but while we were staying in New York the hotel caught on fire. No one was hurt, but the thought of what could have happened cured me of ever taking students on such a field trip again.

Narcissistic, entitled attitudes are crippling schools and American society. We have become a nation of "high maintenance" individuals. Narcissism is said to be the fastest growing mental illness in the United States and is the pathology of our time. This is fostering an erosion in a sense of duty and responsibility and causing a rise in self-gratification, selfishness, and personal, rather than social, awareness.[3] It is also creating a fear of aging, emotional detachment, self-obsession, anxiety, feelings of emptiness, depression, boredom, inadequacy, self-aggrandizement, and low self-esteem.[4]

Most of us today face our world with apprehension and suspicion. Bureaucratization, globalization, and uncertainties surrounding personal relationships and life in general, preoccupy us and our government, causing even greater self-obsession.[5] Strong social ties among individuals and groups within a society are needed to ensure that a society is healthy. Without these connections, alienation and distrust increase.[6] Our predicament is a struggle between narcissism and humanism—between narrow "self-love" and the broader awareness of the interdependency of all mankind.[7]

In the 1970s psychologists and analysts began to report increasing symptoms of pathological narcissism among patients and began to diagnose them as having 'Narcissistic Personality Disorder' (NPD).[8] Social psychologists and sociologists linked the apparent increase to an underlying pattern of social and cultural change. Christopher Lasch in his book *The Culture of Narcissism: American Life in An Age of Diminishing Expectations* claimed that the diagnosis provided an accurate portrait of the "liberated" personality of modern times even though no empirical evidence supported the belief. He believed that an increasingly liberal, secular, affluent, and consumer post-war American society had led to the development of a new narcissistic personality type.[9]

Many people in today's American society perceive reality solely in subjective, private terms. The broader world around them has meaning only as an extension of themselves and their private lives. Such an attitude can become a problem because individuals need to grow beyond their own private lives (with its wants and needs) to participate as members of a community or cohesive society (with its broader wants and needs).[10]

American society was founded on two major core values— freedom and equality. The Declaration of Independence professed that these were inherent rights. The recipe for American individualism would have to be freedom constrained by equality. The Bill of Rights served to balance freedom of individual action and fundamental equality, with an assumption of "tolerance of others" as part of its edict.[11] The emphasis was on individualism, not on narcissism (individualism taken to an extreme), which restricts individuals' experiences in the world to their own subjective realities that they then project onto others and the world.

Industrialization, with its promise of unlimited progress, would help to transform the emphasis from individualism to narcissism. The domination over nature, material abundance, and unlimited personal freedom would plant the seeds for narcissism. Industrial progress made mankind feel omnipotent and omniscient. When we replaced human and animal energy with mechanical and nuclear energy, and when we substituted the computer for the mind, we were on the way to unlimited production and consumption.[12]

Entrenched in consumerism, many Americans developed insatiable desires for material goods, believing these would give life meaning. Wants became needs. Profit-oriented businesses and corporations, the media, and advertising would encourage such consumption. As Fromm so aptly stated:

> Ours is the greatest social experiment ever made
> to solve the question whether pleasure, (the state
> of "having"), in contrast to wellbeing and joy,
> (the state of "being"), can be a satisfactory answer
> to the problem of human existence.[13] (p. 5).

Insatiable consumerism would lead to egoistic behavior—"I want everything for myself; possessing, not sharing, gives me pleasure; I must become greedy because my aim is having."[14] Also, significant to the shift in American society was the "cultural revolution" originating in the 1960s. In Charles Dickens' classic novel *A Tale of Two Cities*, the author states:

> It was the best of times, it was the worst of times. . .
> it was the season of Light, it was the season of
> Darkness, it was the spring of hope, it was the
> winter of despair. . .[15] (p. 1).

The 1960s was a period of dramatic social and political turmoil and change—exhilarating for some, frightening for others. Psychologists Twenge and Campbell deem the 1960s as the time when the "American flag of self-admiration slowly began to unfurl."[16] Hendrick refers to it as the second "crisis of modernity," which worsened in succeeding decades, exacerbating the vulnerability of children.[17]

The American landscape was rocked by civil rights', women's liberation, and gay and lesbian movements along with affirmative action, *Roe vs Wade,* labor militancy, and widespread industrial unrest.[18] Other self-interest groups included anti-psychiatry activists, claimants' groups, and disability reformers.[19]

As individuals and interest groups increasingly asserted their rights, like adolescents rebelling against their parents, rebellion would regress into an infantile state of self-centeredness. Although changes such as civil rights for minority groups and equal pay for women were long overdue, a pre-occupation with "self-interest" settled over the country. "Individualism" was seen as a virtue, and increasingly violent and intolerant politics became the norm.[20] "Identity politics" would gain prominence in American society.[21] In contrast to their altruistic, future-oriented forebears, the new narcissistic "Me Generation" cared only about "self-gratification now."[22]

Self-interest accelerated throughout the 80s, 90s, and into the twenty-first century, fueled by the media, advertising, and entertainment industries. Popular culture, via these industries, encouraged vanity, glamour, and youthfulness. Face lifts, liposuction, breast augmentation, hair transplants, penile enhancements, drugs for erectile dysfunction, personal trainers, and diets—all encouraged people to dip into the "fountain of youth" and self-indulgence.

Movie stars dominated the scene and became role models. TV shows such as *Entertainment Tonight, Access Hollywood*, and *Inside Edition* allowed Americans to become voyeurs to their lives. Individuals could play starring roles in reality TV shows such as *Survivor, The Biggest Loser, Fear Factor, Wife Swap, American Idol, America's Got Talent*, and *Amazing Race.* If you couldn't make it onto one of these shows, you could star on You Tube, Facebook, My Space, or even your cellphone. Such self-indulgent, self-absorbed behavior is rampant, encouraging an extroverted, shallow, and materialistic form of narcissism.[23]

These pursuits don't encourage individuals to take authentic responsibility for life. Most renowned spiritual leaders would suggest that true meaning and understanding of life is an inward journey into the quiet recesses of the soul, without audience participation.

The erosion of American society has taken the greatest toll on the family, parenting, and children. Since the early 70s, divorce rates began to climb, reaching an all-time high of 47% in 2000. The number of day care centers also increased as women joined the work force, liberating themselves from the role of "housewife." Many parents of today's children know only what they experienced as children and are carrying within them the emotional turmoil experienced from living in broken homes and living in an entitlement society.[24]

Some parents project their own dislocated feelings onto their children, taking pains to remove suffering from their children's lives. In doing so, they have become over-protective, over-controlling, and over-compensatory.[25] The result is "sanitized childhoods" for many children who aren't allowed to experiment or make mistakes. Rather, these children seek a "beeline" towards success, jumping over the process of getting there, which should include trial and error, feeling bad sometimes, and learning to cope with disappointment and failure.

Parenting today is often like "raising royalty." The core cultural values of self-admiration and positive feelings have led parents to seek after their children's approval and to do everything to make them happy. Although the intensions are well-meaning, parental pride has reinforced cultural narcissism.[26] Psychologist Polly Young-Eisendreth says that too many modern parents are innocently making the mistake of idealizing their children instead of loving them.[27] We have veered too far toward obeying and pleasing our children rather than helping them have a healthy desire to please their parents. We are too indulgent—giving our kids too much and demanding too little of them. Over-indulging kids can lead to fostering qualities such as laziness, greediness, envy, exaggerated self-esteem, self-righteous indignation, and intolerance of others.[28]

Many children are given the "starring roles in the family drama," and "Alpha Moms" and "Moms to the Max" seek to perfect motherhood, seeing themselves as responsible for perfecting their children. These mothers over-enroll their children in activities, engineering serendipity and spontaneity out of their experiences. They are raising children who want it all, believe they deserve it all, and have unrealistic fantasies about wealth, power, celebrity, and achievement.[29] Parenting has become a confusing mixture of over-indulgence, over-protection, and over-control.

Allthough this is the parenting style in many families across the nation, it is not the case in all families. Parenting varies, covering a range of styles, from those who are over-indulgent and over-protective to those who are strict, or lax, or negligent, or abusive, or a combination of behaviors. However, the focus of this chapter is on that of the over-indulgent, over-protective, and over-controlling parent.

The devastating effects of such parenting practices are being felt within the education system. Teachers' professionalism is being eroded because teachers' opinions hold little weight in the scheme of things. Students and parents are considered the major stakeholders in education, and their opinions and demands far out-weigh those of the teachers, who used to be considered the trained professionals.

One teacher, who gave up teaching to become a psychologist, recounted how she had planned a field trip for her second graders to visit an exhibit at a museum that related to what they were studying in class. They would have lunch in the park afterwards, and parents were invited to participate. Plans for the trip were almost finalized when a group of mothers came to tell the teacher that they had decided on a different field trip for the kids because they thought the museum would be too boring. They proceeded to dictate to her the details of the alternative trip. In frustration, the teacher decided to cancel the trip because she was tired of parent interference in her classroom.

Several years ago, a girl who had been accepted into my year-long drama production class decided halfway through the year to drop out, even though she and her parents had signed a letter at the beginning of the school year agreeing to a year-long commitment. She didn't talk to me about her decision. I knew that she had done so only when I saw her name deleted from my attendance roster. When I spoke to the counselor, she said that she had told the girl to speak with me first to get my approval, which, of course, she hadn't done.

The counselor and I talked to the girl, who admitted that she wanted to drop out because she didn't get a big role in the fall play. I explained that she knew from the beginning that everyone had to audition for roles and that the students who didn't get big parts in the fall play would have first consideration for the spring production. I also stated that when she signed the contract she knew she had made a year-long commitment to the class. I explained that it was important for her to learn to take responsibility for the decisions she makes.

The girl stood her ground, stating that her mother had given her permission to drop the class. When she left the room, the counselor told me that we had no other recourse than to allow the girl to drop because that was the principal's policy. In exasperation, I went to the principal and explained that I felt that it wasn't good policy to allow students to renege on their commitments because it was teaching them to be irresponsible. He agreed but allowed the girl to drop the class anyway.

A retired teacher's frustration at having to "indulge" students and parents was driven home when I spoke to her at a Halloween party in 2011. She came dressed as "a teacher" with pens sticking out of the pockets of her blouse and pants and hand-written notes from parents composed from classroom memories such as:

> Please walk Sharon to the cafeteria at lunch time, help her fit through the door, and be sure no one puts anything green on her plate.

> How dare you expect Frances to read—he is only in the seventh-grade.

> My son wrote his name on his paper and then our dog peed on it and I don't think he should have to fill out a pink slip.

> Braithwaite tells me you are cross-eyed—please quit looking at him that way as it tears at his self-esteem.

> You spoke sternly to Ogden yesterday when he walked across the student tables during that ridiculous test. He told us he was just trying to let off some steam so he could concentrate on the stupid test.

> What's the matter with you people—my son had twelve minutes of homework last night—which upset

him because it took time away from playing video
games with Ivan in Russia.

What do you mean you can't read Emma's paper?
Isn't that your job?

While everyone at the party laughed at the ridiculousness of these notes, the teachers among the group knew that such notes were sadly all too true.

Many students believe they should have special privileges and special exemptions from normal classroom demands, and they often have poor work ethics and little concern for how their behavior affects others.[30] A culture of "entitlement learning" consists of some students believing that they are entitled to high grades just because they attend classes and complete the requirements.[31] Such "academic entitlement" may be a coping strategy for some for dealing with pressures from parents. Repercussions for educators who don't give into student demands are often negative student evaluations or parental intervention on behalf of their children to gain the outcome the parents and/or students feel they deserve. The dilemma for teachers is that they are expected to show "student growth" in their subject areas, but how can teachers show accurate growth when their classrooms are being hijacked by students' and parents' demands? One teacher said she had a student in fifth-grade who tended to be a dreamer during class time, accomplishing little work. At a conference the mother told her that her son was a genius and that the work bored him. (When the teacher checked the boy's intelligence testing scores, she found that he was in the "average" range.)

The mother wanted the teacher to stimulate her son's interest by altering the work to games that he could play. The other kids did the work unaltered but wondered why he got to play games while they had to work.

A parent of an eighth-grade student who had made it into an auditioned choir class phoned the teacher to say that she didn't want her daughter singing religious songs—never mind that the basis of a lot of choir music is spiritual/religious in nature and that the teacher was not planning to preach religion to the students. She wanted to enlighten them to a variety of musical styles and instill in them an appreciation for the roots of most vocal music.

A parent of a sixth-grade student explained to a French teacher that her daughter spoke fluent French because they had lived in France for five years. She wanted the teacher to develop a separate curriculum for the girl since the girl's only option at the sixth-grade level was to take beginning French conversation.

Students should have some sense of independence as they step into the adult world. However, colleges are increasingly reporting that the days of parents dropping off students on campus and waving goodbye are long gone.[32] The number of parents who persistently hover around their children during orientation is rising, which may hamper efforts to help new students begin the transition to life away from home.[33] Some seventeen hundred educators who were surveyed claimed that the number one problem they face today is interfering parents whom they refer to as "helicopter," "snow plow," "kami kazi," or "machinery of heavy lifting" parents. These children are "teacup kids" who are fragile and shatter easily because they don't know how to take responsibility, make decisions, or solve problems.[34]

Colleges are responding in a number of ways. Some professors are writing scholarly articles on the situation, suggesting that more research needs to be done to investigate the detrimental effects of narcissism and entitlement on children and young adults. About 70% of the nation's four-year colleges and universities are hiring "parent coordinators" to organize campus events for the annual parent weekends; produce regular newsletter; staff telephone hotlines; field questions on financial aid, academic issues, homesickness, and helping students to wake up in time for classes.[35] The University of Vermont is training students to be "parent bouncers" to keep parents at bay when new students register for classes.[36]

Consensus doesn't exist about how to solve the problem. Meanwhile, many children face increased psychological distress. They are stuck in "endless adolescence" with a fear of making mistakes, a fear of failure, and an unwillingness to take risks, which robs them of identity, meaning, and a sense of mastery.[37] Many children suffer from depression, feelings of emptiness, boredom, lack of realistic perceptions of themselves, lack of empathy, high pursuit of pleasure, disinterest in work of any kind, and a distorted sense of their importance in the world.[38] Other symptoms include: obsessive self-focus, restless dissatisfaction, pressure to be exceptional, unrealistic fantasies about their abilities, unreadiness to take on adult responsibilities in an imperfect world, feelings of superiority and/or inferiority, and excessive fears of being humiliated.[39]

Not surprisingly, but alarmingly, many children are being medicated to help them get through childhood. Twenty-one million prescriptions—an increase of over 400% from a decade ago—are being filled each year to "enhance" students' ability to pay attention. Because many children are disconnected from themselves—lacking a fierce internal struggle toward a deeper understanding of themselves—they suffer unfocused anxiety and panic because they cannot even identify their fears. They don't have a strong sense of self because they have not been allowed or encouraged to build one, to struggle, or to take the time for the reflection and introspection necessary for making experiences their own and for forging their own meanings.[40]

In his book *Overschooled but Undereducated: Society's Failure to Understand Adolescence*, John Abbott recounts the story about a struggling butterfly:

> A man seeing a butterfly struggling to break
> out of its out-grown cocoon bent down and
> carefully cut away the strands to set the butterfly
> free. To his dismay it flapped its wings weakly
> for a while, then collapsed and died. A biologist
> later explained that the butterfly needed the struggle
> to develop the strength to enable it to fly. By
> robbing the butterfly of that struggle, the man
> made it too weak to live.[41] (p. xxiii-xxiv).

Similar to the above story, the over-indulgence and over-protection of children is robbing them of their ability to grow into emotionally balanced, autonomous adults. They are becoming too weak to do so.

Child psychologist Dr. Shirley Robbins claims that children are not psychologically ready to be demanding their rights. These demands are often manipulative because children don't have the cognition, judgment, or experience to know what is in their best interest. Such judgment evolves gradually, and it is important for adults to realize this when they allow children to advocate for themselves.[42]

So when presidents, politicians, policymakers, and the public automatically blame teachers for the problems within our education system, they need to think twice about such a judgment. Narcissistic, entitled attitudes are a driving force in the equation, and such attitudes from parents and students are usually given deference in the classroom—to the detriment of teachers and the education of the children.

Solutions to America's narcissism epidemic are complex because the problems lie within the American psyche. Nevertheless, as parents, educators, and adults, we can heed the warning signs. Awareness is the first step towards action. The parents in "The Veldt" gave into Peter and Wendy's demands to have "one more night in the nursery"—unfortunately. And, unfortunately, many schools are perpetuating narcissistic, entitlement behavior by giving into both children's and parents' demands. That is not to say that all children's and parents' requests are unreasonable and/or developmentally or educationally unsound, because many are not. Reasonable requests should be honored.

Today's children are tomorrow's leaders. Will they be ready to lead? And, where are we headed—as a society—if they are not? After all, it is we who created this troubling "culture of narcissism," and it is we who need to heed the warning signs if we are ever going to turn back the unrealistic tide of entitlement. Returning teachers back into their leadership roles in the classroom is a step in the right direction. They are trained professionals and should be treated as such.

Chapter Four
No Cellphone Left Behind
"Techno-Toiletries Run Rampant"

And the lord said,
"Let there be light, and the TV set came on."

.   **A**ustralian cartoonist Michael Leunig created a cartoon in which his signature character sits in front of the TV set, arm wrapped around his son's shoulder while they watch the sunset on the screen. Outside the window next to them, the actual sun is setting in the distance.[1]

The TV set, the technological miracle of the twentieth century, is an "altar" around which families and friends gather to pay homage and to worship. It's the centerpiece in many, if not most, living rooms and has also become a feature in bedrooms, kitchens, bathrooms, garages, and even cars.

In 1957 when I was five-years-old, the television was a new invention, and I can remember sitting in front of it watching the NBC Nightly News with anchormen Chet Huntley and David Brinkley. While I was too young to understand the news, I was intrigued by the ending of the broadcast. I knew that Chet Huntley was in New York and David Brinkley was in Washington D.C., but each night they would say goodnight to each other, and their faces were on the screen, side by side, at the same time. My five-year-old brain couldn't grasp how they could be together on the screen when they were located in different cities!

I would never have been able to foresee how such technology would come to influence almost every aspect of life. Individuals would eventually carry their own phones wherever they went—talking, texting, taking photos. Instant connection! Constant contact! Cars would be fitted with TV sets, DVD players, and navigation systems. People would have garage openers, sensitized outdoor and indoor lighting systems, security cameras, and remote controls, to name a few. In another Michael Leunig cartoon the signature character is carrying two TV sets onto an ark while in the foreground two toasters, two microwaves, two telephones, and two motorbikes wait to be carried aboard.[2] A poignant comment on the world we now inhabit.

In 1981, while I was teaching in Australia, Leunig's cartoon of "Noah's Ark" was a topic of conversation in my senior literature class. The discussion centered on the impact of technology on our lives. I challenged the students to see if any of them could go for one week without watching TV. Fifteen students took the challenge, and five of them lasted the week.

In 2011, when No Cellphone Left Behind came into its prime, I had a similar discussion with my eighth-grade drama class. The conversation centered on the impact of the cellphone on our lives. I challenged my eighth-graders to see if any of them could go for one week without using their cellphones. Five students agreed to the challenge, but by the next day all of them had dropped out of the competition. Although these two classroom contests are not scientific evidence of the increasing influence of technology on children, I, and other colleagues who have been in education for many years, have been worried about students' increasing obsession with it.

A growing number of writers and researchers from various fields are beginning to worry also. Books with such titles as: *Distracted: The Erosion of Attention and the Coming Dark Age; The Shallows: What the Internet is Doing to Our Brain; The Dumbest Generation; Blown to Bits: Your Life, Liberty, and Happiness After the Digital Explosion; The Age of American Unreason; Failure to Connect: How Computers Affect Our Children's Minds—and What We Can Do About It;* and *Endangered Minds: Why Children Don't Think and What We Can Do About It* warn where we may be heading as a nation if we don't take a critical look at the side effects of technology on young people.

"Techno-toiletries" have become "techno-lifelines" for many in this "plugged in" generation. They are plugged-in not only to TV sets but also to cellphones, computers, and iPod's. Face-to-face contact is not required, and no real human interaction occurs. The press of a button can delete or disconnect whoever is on the other end. The character of "human relationships" has decidedly changed; interactions have become impersonal, inorganic, and one-dimensional with no chance of interpreting body language or tone of voice for accuracy in communication.

In the 1972 film *Being There*, Peter Sellers plays the character Chance Gardener, a man without a family, who has been raised by a wealthy "old gentleman." Chance lives in a bungalow on his benefactor's grounds, looks after the gardens on the estate, and has no contact with the outside world or other human beings except the housekeeper. He is uneducated but is an expert in gardening. His lifeline is his TV set where he has one-dimensional relationships with characters on the screen, whom he can switch off with the click of his remote control. After his benefactor dies, Chance is forced out into the world. Not knowing how to relate to people, he uses his remote control in an attempt to switch them off when encounters aren't to his liking. His only conversation revolves around platitudes describing gardening, which are misinterpreted to be profound political statements about the state of American society. Chance rises to national prominence when the president of the United States defers to him for economic and political advice. The final scene of the movie has Chance "walking on water" across a lake, while the quote "Life is a state of mind" is superimposed in the background.[3]

The humor of *Being There* is the seemingly ridiculousness of the situation. Yet, considering the extent our world has become technological, it's not really that far from reality. Today's youth may be Chance Gardeners in the making who, like Chance, cannot communicate meaningfully, yet will be ignorantly elevated to our leadership!

The give-and-take of friendships and relationships has increasingly taken an abbreviated form via cellphone texting, instant messaging, Facebook walls, and MySpace bulletins. The Pew Research Center found that half of American teenagers between the ages of twelve and seventeen send fifty or more texts a day! One-third send more than one hundred a day! Additionally, they spend approximately one-and-a-half hours text messaging and half-an-hour talking on their cellphones each day.[4] Moreover, the average kid absorbs two-and-a-half hours of music each day, five hours of TV and movies, three hours of internet and video games, but only thirty-eight minutes of reading, according to a study by the Kaiser Family Foundation—a total of seventy-five hours of media each week. Kids can even watch TV on their laptops or on their cellphones. About half of the heaviest media users get C's or lower in school, while only a quarter of light users receive bad grades.[5]

Beyond the grades, Bauerlein, in his book *The Dumbest Generation: How the Digital Age Stupefies Young Americans and Jeopardizes Our Future*, explores how the digital age is stupefying American youth and jeopardizing our future as a nation. He observes that the new habitus of the Digital Age is of youth undergoing an intense awareness of one another, with their social lives ruling them. They don't want to be "left behind" by their peers, so they have to tune in and turn on via e-mails, text messages, blog postings and comments, phone calls, tweets, feeds, photos, and songs. Many leave their cellphones on all night, set to wake them in case they receive a text message or Facebook posting during the night.[6]

All of us need alone time—time for the silent spaces of the soul to speak to us of personal lessons that cannot be learned in a classroom. Many parents I have spoken to are despairing and frustrated that their children are swept up in a technological world. These "screenagers" feel peer pressure to have the latest cellphones, iPods, and computer technology, and their parents feel compelled to give them what makes them happy. Consequently, the people "left behind" are parents and teachers who no longer have the influence necessary to help them become discerning, responsible adults and citizens.

The more kids are immersed in contacting each other every minute of every day, the less they listen to adults, who should be the ones mentoring them into adulthood. It's easier to blame teachers for students' lack of learning or to mandate more testing and data collection than it is to investigate how social networking and digital technology may be impacting students intellectually and emotionally, impinging on their abilities to learn or to want to learn. In fact, formal education may be becoming irrelevant to many of them.

Educational psychologist Dr. Janet Healy, in her book *Failure to Connect: How Computers Affect Our Children's Minds—and What we can Do About It,* states that technology shapes the growing mind; the younger the mind, the more malleable it is. She believes that we are exposing young people to new "digital teachers and playmates" without carefully and fully considering the effects. The assumption is that the use of technology at home and at school will enrich children's minds and improve the quality of learning to the benefit of society and the world. Major corporations, the public in general, and government officials often give unquestioning support to such assumptions. However, Healy states that no convincing proof exists showing that technology will achieve these results. She questions whether we are grasping at a technological "quick fix" to solve complicated problems within the education system that we have failed to address or have overlooked.[7]

Some psychologists and experts worry whether technology may even be changing the nature of kids' friendships. They question whether kids are becoming more connected and supportive of their friends or are losing intimacy and the emotional give-and-take derived from regular, extended face-to-face relating. People who study relationships believe that childhood friendships are important for building trusting relationships outside of the family, laying the foundation for healthy adult relationships:

> In this highly "connected" world, children are not
> developing sound interpersonal skills. Communication
> by IM, text messaging, or e-mail is often a shorthand
> means of relating. Children aren't learning the nuances
> of interpersonal dialogue and therefore are lacking
> sensitivity in relationships. . . . It may not be accidental
> that aggression in schools is on the rise, considering
> the fact that children are not learning the nuances
> of reading facial gestures, understanding tone of voice,
> and retracting or backing down when miscommun-
> ication or misperceptions occur.[8] (p. 81).

Today's youth may well fail to develop empathy and fail to learn to read the emotional nuances and social cues such as facial expression and body language that are important to human communication.

In some schools, students are turning up for classes to find that teachers have been replaced by computers offering on-line modes of education, with lab technicians as the only facilitators. In the Miami-

Dade County public schools, seven thousand students are enrolled in classrooms with no teachers. They may have found a much cheaper way to deliver education but at a cost to the students. Schools are often the only place where many students can learn how to deal with complicated issues in life or learn how to develop relationships with other people. Since teachers are role models for such learning, undoubtedly there will be intrinsic costs if such modes of education become the rule rather than the exception. Of course, billionaire corporate entrepreneurs such as Bill Gates stand to make millions in profits selling such online courses to schools.[9]

A curious consequence of burgeoning technology occurred among students in my drama classes. Using non-realistic theater techniques to create dream sequences, we began the project by talking about dreams and what they represent; then students would recount their dreams to the class. Over the years, students have increasingly had dreams revolving around technology.

One student said that he once fell asleep in the car and dreamed that he was listening to his iPod. Another said that he was a Webkin frog named Carl inside the virtual Webkin game. Another still, said that she was inside a virtual game called Kingdom of Hearts finding creatures called Heartlets. Technology is definitely a part of children's lives, so it makes sense that they will have dreams about the technology they use. However, it's fascinating to note that not only are they having dreams, but are participating in dreams within dreams—virtual games are not real, yet they dream that they are part of the games. The gestalt of what it means to dream appears to be shifting. So, too, is the gestalt of what it means to be human and how we perceive reality or how we live it.

In *The Evolution of Consciousness: The Origin of the Way We Think*, Robert Ornstein claims that the human mind functions in the way that it does because the world around it was a certain way for some forty thousand years. He states that the ancestral system of biological adaptation flourished when the world was gradually evolving at a stable rate. However, it took about a million years to produce the first billion humans, then only fourteen years to produce another billion. So, he claims that no one is biologically prepared to view fifteen thousand murders before puberty. No one is biologically prepared for the crowds, the noise, the pollution, and the rapid technological development that is occurring in the modern world. In the past, the change in life's complexity was gradual enough to accommodate the Stone Age, the Iron Age, writing, printing, farming, the early Industrial Revolution, and the Atomic Age.[10]

Human inventiveness is overwhelming human adaptability, and our ability to judge is lagging behind our ability to create. We may have reached a crossroads in our intellectual and cultural evolution—a transition into a new way of thinking and of "being" in the world. "Yesterday's mind"—a linear thought process that has been calm, focused, and undistracted over millennia—may be evolving into a new kind of mind that wants and needs to process information in short, disjointed, overlapping bursts.[11]

In her book *Distracted: The Erosion of Attention and the Coming Dark Age,* Maggie Jackson argues:

> Amid the glittering promise of our new technologies
> and the wondrous potential of our scientific gains,
> we are nurturing a culture of social diffusion,
> intellectual fragmentation, sensory detachment. In
> this new world something is amiss. And that
> something is attention. . . .The way we live is eroding
> our capacity for deep, sustained, perceptive attention—
> the building block of intimacy, wisdom, and cultural
> progress.[12] (p.13).

Jackson queries whether we are redefining "intelligence" and "intimacy and trust," failing to notice the "deeper, human costs" in our adaptation to a technological world of "twitch-speed, multitasking, and bullet-point" relating.[13]

Jackson states that "paying attention" is part of human nature. Similar to our respiratory and circulatory systems, "paying attention" is part of survival. It is a key to higher forms of thinking, to our morality, and to our overall happiness. She claims that "attention" consists of three networks related to awareness, focus, and planning; and, that the system of attention is directly related to "complex cognitive and emotional operations," especially for resolving conflicts between different areas of the brain.[14]

Philosopher and psychologist William James defined attention as "the taking possession of the mind, in clear and vivid form, of one out of what may seem several, simultaneously possible objects or trains of thought. It implies withdrawal from some things in order to deal effectively with others. Attention allows individuals to regulate their focus and impulses and engage in planning."[15]

Attention also creates flow in life. Research has shown that people who can focus report less fear, frustration, and sadness because their minds aren't flitting from idea to idea or task to task. These individuals are better able to process their thoughts and feelings, then let them go.[16]

Today's children are technologically savvy at multi-tasking. They learn that they can watch TV, text friends on their cellphones, listen to their iPod's, and do homework at the same time. Such multi-tasking, however, affects their cognitive performance because it requires the brain to perform sequential processing by switching attention back and forth between tasks. When an individual's attention is divided, the ability to accomplish complex tasks (such as homework assignments) and to do higher-level thinking is reduced. Such multi-tasking is rewiring the brains of our youth from an early age.

Neuroscientists and psychologists of the twentieth century have developed an understanding of the complexity of the human brain, especially its neuroplasticity. Previously, the brain was thought to be an unchanging concrete structure. However, researchers uncovered experiments dating back to William James and Sigmund Freud that illustrate the brain's plasticity, meaning that the brain can alter its functioning so that humans can adapt to the world around them and develop new skills for survival.

According to Alvaro Pascual-Leone, a top neurology researcher at Harvard Medical School, as quoted in Nicholas Carr's book *The Shallows: What the Internet Is Doing to Our Brain*:

> Plasticity is the normal ongoing state of the nervous
> system throughout the life span. Our brains are
> constantly changing in response to our experiences
> and our behavior, reworking their circuitry with each
> sensory input, motor act, association, reward signal,
> action plan, or (shift of) awareness. Neuroplasticity
> is one of the most important products of evolution,
> a trait that enables the nervous system to escape the
> restrictions of its own genome and thus adapt to

environmental pressures, physiologic changes, and experiences.[17] (p. 379).

The discovery of the brain's neuroplasticity has led to new treatments for individuals suffering from brain injuries, and it has made us aware of the brain's flexibility when learning new skills and adapting to change.

However, the brain's neuroplasticity also leads to creation of new circuits. Once these new circuits are formed by repetition of new physical or mental activity, the brain wants to keep exercising the circuits it has formed—to fine-tune its operation. Fine-tuning can, ironically, lock human beings into rigid behaviors. Routine activities are done more rapidly and efficiently, and unused circuits atrophy. So, the brains of our youth may be being rewired so that they are losing the ability to focus, to process thoughts and feelings, or to develop critical thinking skills. As politicians, policy-makers, educators, and the public consider extending technology into the American classroom, there needs to be thoughtful discussion as to what detrimental effects it may have on the learning process.[18]

The younger the child, the more plastic the brain. The more a child uses technology at a young age, the stronger the synapses (connections) become within the brain, making the connections automatic and harder to change as the child grows older. If age-appropriate use of technology isn't considered or monitored by parents and schools, the brain can build resistant habits that interfere with academic learning.[19] Research has found that excessive exposure to various forms of media (TV, cellphone, computer, iPod) negatively affects children's school performance and performance on standardized achievement tests because, rather than spending time reading or focusing on alternative school-related activities, kids spend time multi-tasking via their electronic media. Children's writing is often similar in style to television scripts or to text messages, which are fragmented and disconnected with no regard for logic. According to Jackson:

> Nearly a third of fourteen- to twenty-one year-olds
> juggle five to eight media while doing homework.
> Yet for all their tech fluency, kids show less patience,
> skepticism, tenacity, and skill than adults in navigating

the Web, all while overestimating their prowess, studies show. Meanwhile, U.S. fifteen-year-olds rank twenty-forth out of twenty-nine developed countries on an Organization for Economic Cooperation and Development (OECD) test of problem-solving skills related to analytic reasoning—the sort of skills demanded in today's workforce. . . .Government and other studies show that many U.S. high school students can't synthesize or assess information, express complex thoughts, or analyze arguments.[20] (p. 18).

Bloom's Taxonomy has underpinned education for years. It identifies the stages of cognition that individuals need to develop to be able to comprehend, analyze, apply, synthesize, and evaluate information. Individuals need to be able to apply this process to their personal lives and to issues within their communities and society at large. If we are creating a distracted population whose main desire is to multi-task and flit from one form of media to the next, without being able to focus on any one thing, what sort of a society are we creating? We live in a complex world with complex problems, so we need individuals who can think through issues to form sound judgments. If we are educating children who are unable to express complex thoughts, analyze arguments, and synthesize ideas, the future of the United States as a democracy is in jeopardy.

Reading is one of the most important skills a child needs because it develops the thinking process described in Bloom's Taxonomy, and it creates a literate society:

Literacy is absolutely necessary for the development not only of science but also of history, philosophy, explicative understanding of literature and of any art, and indeed for the exploration of language (including oral speech) itself. The ability to write is utterly invaluable and indeed essential for the realization of fuller, interior, human potentials. Writing heightens consciousness.[21] (p. 57).

However, multi-tasking and reading hypertext on computer screens creates individuals who are often no longer interested in reading. Instead, they are learning to skim rather than to ponder texts for their complex meaning.

A 2007 report from the U.S. Department of Education found that twelfth graders' scores on three different kinds of reading tests— performing a task, gathering information, and literary experience— fell between 1992 and 2005. Literary aptitude showed the largest drop—a drop of twelve pecent.[22] A 2008 U.S. Bureau of Labor Statistics report states that the average time spent reading by Americans over the age of fourteen has fallen to one hundred and thirty-three minutes a week, which is a drop of 11% since 2004. And young people between the ages of twenty-five and thirty-four (the most avid net users) read an average of forty-nine minutes a week— down 29% from 2004.[23] Only 30% of college graduates can understand information on a food label—down from 40% a decade ago. Also, approximately 57% of Americans don't read a single book a year.[24]

Reading can develop the skill of deep concentration and attention because an individual has to focus on a single task— and such focus strengthens the neural links needed to counter distractedness. The reading of a sequence of printed pages requires readers to make associations, draw inferences and analogies, and develop their own ideas—the stuff of critical thinking and of creating a literate and literary brain:[25]

> The words of the writer act as a catalyst on the mind
> of the reader, inspiring new insights, associations,
> and perceptions, sometimes even epiphanies. The
> world of the written word enhances and deepens
> people's critical thinking skills and level of
> consciousness and understanding of themselves,
> of life, of the world around them.[26] (p. 55).

To become a fluent reader, a child must begin the process of reading at a young age so that identifying words becomes automatic, or the child will never learn to explore a text's meaning. The child must be able to focus and use the skill of attention to learn the basics of letter-sound connections in a word. Doing so causes neural pathways between the visual and phonological areas involved in reading. Thus, a child must learn not only to decode words, but through the power of attention, to drill this activity into the brain. Only then can the child advance to the next levels of reading which involve comprehension, analysis, synthesis, and application of what has been read.[27] Psychologist Janet Healy believes that with the development of attention in early reading, children develop important habits of mind—sustained concentration, language, imagery, and questioning strategies.[28]

In the late 1980s, when computers were beginning to transform the classroom, experts thought that reading hypertext with links would enrich the reader's cognitive skills. However, research studies began to show that it didn't. A 1989 study showed that reading hypertext on computers increased the reader's cognitive load, weakening comprehension and retention of what is being read because the reader is absorbed in evaluating links and navigating through them, dividing his attention and focus. Readers of hypertext tend to click through pages rather than read them, whereas, people who read linear text comprehend, remember, and learn.[29]

In another study conducted in 2000, researchers had people read two articles about opposing learning theories.[30] Each article was set up in the same way with similar headings and with links to each other, allowing readers to jump from one article to the other. The researchers hypothesized that readers who used the links would gain a deeper understanding of the theories and their differences than would people who read the theories sequentially, reading first one, then the other. The test subjects who read the pages linearly scored significantly higher on a comprehension test than did those who clicked back and forth between the pages.

In 2005, psychologists Le Fevre and DeStefano conducted a review of thirty-eight past experiments involving reading of hypertext. Most evidence showed that reading performance was impaired because of the visual processing required in the reading of hypertext and the increased demands of decision-making. They concluded that many features of hypertext increased cognitive load, which may require working memory capacity that exceeds readers' capabilities.[31]

Technology has also made attendance-taking a crazy ordeal in many classrooms. One of the latest technological developments is a computer application that immediately informs parents throughout the day if their child has not attended a class. Teachers are expected to take attendance at the beginning of classes. Students often show up late for various reasons: negotiating jammed lockers, being released late from other classes, attending meetings with counselors, talking to other teachers, or being called to the office. If a child doesn't show up during the first ten minutes of class when the teacher takes attendance, the computer application texts or phones the parents and leaves a message.

Panicky parents then call the school wondering where their children are. Then, the teacher often gets a phone call from the attendance clerk during her lessons to verify a student's absence or to ask why the teacher hasn't changed the absence to a tardy if the student showed up late to class. One day I received a call asking why I had marked a student absent who was at school. I explained that I didn't mark the student absent. The student had transferred into my class that day, and her name hadn't yet been added to my computer roster. I suggested that the teacher whose class she had transferred from probably marked the girl absent because her name was still on that teacher's roster, but she wasn't in her classroom. I also had a situation where a student was sitting in class, but when I took roll she had already been marked absent by the office, and I couldn't change the attendance record on my computer. I e-mailed the attendance clerk to say that the student was sitting in my class.

Nevertheless, we have evolved to where we are; so, maybe we will be able to adapt to the current technological world we have created. In the worst case scenario, we might no longer need to use cognition or emotions to survive.

We might become like robots or automatons in the technological, sound-bite, "brave new world" we have created; quick reactions, without thought, may be all that is needed to survive. As Nicholas Carr observes in *The Shallows*, the irony of the situation is that the computers that we program have now begun to program us.[32]

Research suggests that as the brain grows in response to its environment, it becomes "custom-tailored" to that environment. Thus, a technological environment can expand or dull various mental skills, depending on how the technology is used. The more actively children use their minds as they interact with technology, the more active their learning habits will develop. Unfortunately, with today's software this is not always the case.[33]

Even so, many individuals and schools believe that computers and schools don't mix. Waldorf schools around the country adhere to an education philosophy focused on physical activity and learning through creative, hands-on tasks. The Waldorf philosophy believes that computers inhibit creativity, movement, human interaction, and attention span. Ironically, the chief technology officer of e-Bay and employees of Silicon Valley giants like Google, Apple, Yahoo, and Hewlett-Packard send their kids to Waldorf schools! The chief teaching tools for these kids are such things as pens and paper, knitting needles, and occasionally, mud! Alan Eagle, who holds a computer science degree from Dartmouth and works in executive communications at Google, sends his daughter to a Waldorf school. He states that he rejects the idea that students need technology aids in grammar school![34]

Now is a critical time to evaluate the American education system. Educators and policymakers need to review the current research concerning the effects of technology on the young. They need to discern the possible "hidden agendas" of such groups as corporations which may have vested interests in the research they promote. The issue is far more complex than targeting "ineffective" teachers and blaming them for children's lack of success in school.

Chapter Five
No Censorship Left Behind
"See No Evil, Hear No Evil, Speak No Evil"

"**P**olitical correctness" has probably impacted the American education system more than any other social issue in the last thirty years. Perceived discrimination against certain political, social, or economic groups has led to many "entitlement policies" that serve to reinforce a legalistic and litigious society. If you say anything "wrong" in America today, you could be sued, penalized, or fired.

When I first returned to the United States from Australia, I felt as though I had walked into an Orwellian drama. *Nineteen Eighty-four* first caught my attention during high school in 1969. The world of Big Brother, Newspeak, Doublethink, and the Thought Police transported me into an inconceivable future society where an insidious totalitarian regime ruled via the use of propaganda and mind control. Big Brother watched every move of its citizens, and history and language were manipulated in a calculated effort to control individuals' knowledge, thoughts, feelings, speech, and actions.[1]

I had read the book at a time of great cultural upheaval and transformation in the United States. An upheaval "of the people, by the people, and for the people" that railed at the traditional institutions that had bound individuals and groups with cords of racism and sexism. It was a time of personal liberation. To a youth embroiled in this revolution, Orwell's novel was merely an improbable work of science fiction, only fitting of China's Cultural Revolution taking place at the same time. China's revolution was perpetrated by Mao and his Red Guard with the goals of halting capitalist elements that were creeping into China's socialist regime. Mao's revolution sought to alter education, literature and art, and other aspects of Chinese society that did not correspond to the socialist economic base and development of the socialist system.[2]

So I shelved *Nineteen Eighty-four* until I was teaching college prep English in Australia in the year 1984, and Orwell's controversial novel was on the syllabus. It was exciting to revisit literature I had read when I was the same age as my students. The students found the book difficult to comprehend because, similar to me at their age, they lived in a democratic country and were relatively free to have their own thoughts, feelings, and opinions. Also, they didn't have the life experience yet to understand Orwell's perceptions about the world of power, politics, and government.

The novel presented my students with an understanding of what it would be like to lose the freedoms that they all cherished and helped them realize that they play a role in ensuring that Australia remains a democratic country. Participating in the democratic process required not only that they be informed, but also that they examine the integrity of the information being presented so they could make thoughtful decisions. Re-reading the book affirmed what I had early on believed was my role as an English teacher—that of giving students the critical thinking skills they needed for becoming discerning adults. I wanted to give them the tools for learning to think deeply and divergently. Through literature and class discussions, I wanted to take them beyond their own personal life experiences to explore ideas and worlds beyond themselves.

According to leading education historian Diane Ravitch, in her timely book *The Language Police*, textbook publishers and state education agencies even now work to rid textbooks, national and state tests, classrooms, and library materials of racist, sexist, and elitist language. What may have begun with good intentions has gone to an extreme. Ravitch states:

> After many years of studying the history of education
> and writing about the politics of education, I discovered
> some things that shocked me. Almost by accident, I
> stumbled upon an elaborate, well-established protocol of
> beneficent censorship, quietly endorsed and broadly

implemented by textbook publishers, testing agencies, professional associations, states, and the federal government. . .Educational materials are now governed by an intricate set of rules to screen out language and topics that might be considered controversial or offensive. Some of this censorship is trivial, some is ludicrous, and some is breathtaking in its power to dumb down what children learn in schools.[4] (p. 3).

Ravitch discusses the elaborate process that textbook publishers and test-writing committees apply to effectively remove language or ideas that might offend anyone. Having been on President Clinton's voluntary national test committee in 1998, Ravitch despairs at how bias and sensitivity review has become a detailed and accepted code of censorship that is widely practiced but is hidden from the public.

While on the committee, she and its other members had hoped that reading material for the test would be of a high standard based on good literature. It was not. Disillusioned, she researched the textbook and testing industries and discovered that nationwide bias and sensitivity concerns were the focus of both industries' guidelines. Textbooks and tests had to be designed to leave out any language or material that might upset students and/or fail to take into account their specific backgrounds. They had to avoid language, symbols, words, phrases, or examples that were deemed sexist, racist, offensive, inappropriate, or negative toward any group. They also had to avoid subject matter on tests that might be considered "controversial or emotionally charged." It was strongly suggested that any literary or historical passages before 1970 be excluded because they were likely to contain "inappropriate" language and subject matter.[5] Thus, important examples of classical Literature, actual events, and historical documents were "left behind" in a bid to placate interest groups and protect students from offense—or to protect the adults within these interest groups from having to deal with the complexities of an imperfect world.

Banned topics often included such controversial issues as politics, religion, slavery/race relations, poverty, sexuality, euthanasia, suicide, AIDS, evolution, and drugs.[6] Twenty-five of the most controversial books often under the censorship knife from 1965 to the early 1980s included:

The Adventures of Huckleberry Finn by Mark Twain
The Diary of a Young Girl by Anne Frank
Black Like Me by John Howard Griffin
Brave New World by Aldous Huxley
The Catcher in the Rye by J. D. Salinger
The Electric Kool-Aid Acid Test by Tom Wolfe
A Farewell to Arms by Ernest Hemingway
Go Ask Alice, anonymous
The Good Earth by Pearl Buck
The Grapes of Wrath by John Steinbeck
I Know Why the Caged Bird Sings by Maya Angelou
Johnny Got His Gun by Dalton Trumbo
The Learning Tree by Gordon Parks
Lord of the Flies by William Golding
Love Story by Erich Segal
Manchild in the Promised Land by Claude Brown
My Darling, My Hamburger by Paul Zindel
1984 by George Orwell
Of Mice and Men by John Steinbeck
One Flew Over the Cuckoo's Nest by Ken Kesey
Ordinary People by Judith Guest
The Scarlet Letter by Nathaniel Hawthorne
A Separate Peace by John Knowles
Slaughterhouse-Five by Kurt Vonnegut
To Kill a Mockingbird by Harper Lee[7] (p. 74-75).

The absurdity of the bias and sensitivity reviews is evident in the samples they rejected. A passage about peanuts was rejected because it suggested that peanuts were nutritious, and a student with a peanut allergy might get distracted by the passage on a test. An historical passage about women and quilting was rejected because, despite its historical accuracy, it presented a stereotype of females. A passage about a young blind man who hiked to the top of Mt. McKinley was rejected because students who lived in areas where there were mountains and hiking would have an advantage on the test over those who didn't live in such areas. (Also, the panel felt that the passage implied that blind people are at a disadvantage in difficult and dangerous situations compared to individuals with normal eye sight.) A biographical excerpt about Gutzon Borglum, who designed Mt. Rushmore, was censored because Mt. Rushmore is offensive to the Lakota Native Americans of the Black Hills.[8]

Bias and sensitivity guidelines began to stipulate specific requirements about what writers could and could not say, listing forbidden words and phrases related to gender bias and stereotyping. Writers were also required to depict both sexes in the same professions and the same activities. California required that writers depict the cultural diversity of American society so that no group would be "left behind." Also, each group must receive proportional representation and must be presented only in a positive light.[9]

Ravitch reviewed a dozen world history textbooks and found that complex events and ideas were simplified because of space requirements or adjusted so history is presented as:

> a story of cultural equivalence: All of the world's
> civilizations were great and glorious, all produced
> grand artistic, cultural, and material achievements,
> and now the world is growing more global and
> interconnected. . .In keeping with the imperative
> of avoiding ethnocentrism, no culture is 'primitive.'
> The idea of progress has disappeared because no
> culture is more or less advanced than any other. . .
> students who learn about the world from these
> texts are unlikely to understand why some civiliza-
> tions flourished and others languished, or why
> people vote with their feet to leave some places and
> go to others. Nor will they know that people in some
> regions have been trapped in grinding poverty for
> generations.[10] (p. 141).

In an attempt to create an ideal society, the world of education, in many ways, has become a world of constriction rather than expansion, a world of indoctrination rather than inquiry. Students are being taught to fit into a narrow and rigid world of censorship rather than to be open-minded about life and the world around them. The American education system has become a socially engineered world that limits the development of students' cognitive skills and abilities. It is manipulated by narcissistic, entitled interest groups that can view life only from their own narrow perspectives. Textbook publishing and testing companies fear being "left behind" if they don't comply with censorship demands.

The assumption driving politically conservative and politically correct language usage and non-controversial reading material is that children won't be racist or sexist if they aren't exposed to racist or sexist language and ideas. Children won't think negative thoughts or do negative things, such as commit crimes, if they aren't exposed to ideas that model such thoughts and behavior.

The most recent attempts at censorship within public education occured in Texas and Colorado. According to journalist Stephanie Simon, in September 2014, the State Board of Education in Texas, which is driven by political conservatives, approved a new set of high school history textbooks, mostly published by major publishing houses, that distorts history and knowledge with the intention of slanting social studies to the political right. School board members—none of whom are experts in history—wanted to alter historical facts to suit their personal and political beliefs. Distortions included such ideas as Moses played a role in writing the American Constitution; the Constitution doesn't include the words "separation between church and state;" segregated schools weren't all that bad; and taxes levied on programs for social security haven't particularly improved society. Other distortions included de-emphasizing major decisions that actually impacted American history, such as the Supreme Court decision that declared enforced prayer in schools unconstitutional in favor of focusing on the arguments and rulings of a lower state court in the case of *Engels vs Vitale* which supported school prayer. Such a focus downplays what the Texas Board of Education doesn't want to hear and eschews what students learn. The focus is on ideology rather than on ideas.[11]

To counter the influence of the politically conservative in public education, the Texas Freedom Network Education Fund asked experts in the field of history to review the textbooks. Their opinions were scathing, as was the opinion of the conservative Fordham Institute think tank that denounced the Texas standards in American history as a "politicized distortion" with "misrepresentations at every turn."[12]

Similar controversy and dissention erupted in September, 2014 in Jeffco school district which is Denver, Colorado's second largest district. Newly elected conservative board member Julie Williams proposed that the school board establish a curriculum review committee to review the district's Advanced Placement American History curriculum. The committee's goal would be to only include historical information that "promotes citizenship, patriotism, the free-market system, and respect for authority and for individual rights while downplaying historical evidence that condones civil disorder, social strife, or disregard for the law."[13]

Hundreds of high school students and teachers actively protested Williams' proposal. Their protests have led to a national debate about censorship which has gained support from the College Board that administers the AP program, the coalition of First Amendment and education group, the American Civil Liberties Union, and the National Coalition Against Censorship. The board has had to come up with an alternative plan which includes input from educators, students, and community members, as well as the district's chief academic officer.[14]

Shouldn't the study of history evoke students to think like historians, to examine original documents and texts that give an in-depth, yet balanced perspective of America's history? A perspective that draws from a variety of events that created the U.S.'s rich history, presenting ideas not ideology? True education asks individuals to use higher level thinking skills to formulate conclusions, not to memorize a canned interpretation of someone's biased reality. Also, censoring aspects of history with the goal of creating citizens who are respectful of authority is an ineffective, abstract approach to solving the problem.

Rather, children and adolescents need a more immediate, personal, and practical way to learn such behavior. They need parents and teachers who are prepared, and/or allowed, to set limits and boundaries on children's behavior and to follow through with consequences so that they learn that their actions have repercussions and that they can't always do whatever they want to do. As I mentioned in a previous chapter, children's rights have gone too far. Treating children as if they are equal to adults—which is the current *modus operandi* in many homes and schools today—is doing them an injustice and American society a disservice. Setting boundaries and giving consequences from a young age teaches children self-discipline, responsibility, and respect, whether it be for themselves or others. This will ultimately lead to an understanding of the more abstract principle of respect for country and the law.

Also, life abounds with conflict, contradiction, and controversy. Censorship of language and ideas doesn't change the essence of life. It merely limits our ability to teach children to think intelligently and deeply, to give children the cognition needed to deal with the realities of life that will unpredictably come their way. In essence, what we are doing is repressing and dumbing down children. Yet paradoxically, "creativity, critical thinking, and problem solving" are the skills that the 21st Century Learning Policy has mandated as the focus of education in schools across the country. Teachers are expected to demonstrate "student growth" in these areas each year, a Sisyphean task considering the lay of the land, and a task that holds teachers accountable, without considering the dynamics of the situation.

Literature in schools should do more than appeal to students' personal narratives in an attempt to boost their self-esteem while trying not to offend anyone. Otherwise, children become trapped within their own self-referencing, narcissistic bubbles. Literature should enable them to confront life as it is. It should take them beyond the world they live in and beyond the world they perceive. It should beckon them to question, to explore, to feel, to expand. It should call them to delve within their own psyches to more fully and deeply understand life and the world around them. It should invite them to use their imaginations. It should show them how to empathize with other people and how to communicate more effectively. And, that is not to say that "anything goes" when it comes to selecting reading material and content within the classroom. Of course, age appropriate material must be a major consideration in the selection process.

Ravitch states that "We do not know how these trends may yet affect the quality of our politics, our civic life, and our ability to communicate with one another somewhere above the level of the lowest common denominator. The consequences can't be good."[15] After reading her book, I realized that because I had been out of the country for so long, I could more readily identify the consequences.

When I first returned from Australia in 2002 to teach in America, I found students to have narrow senses of entitlement, savvy to the lingo of "political correctness" when they voiced their demands or concerns. An African American student, who monitored everything I said through "politically correct" racial filters, accused me of being racist for playing African music when we were doing rhythm exercises. I told him that it was anything but "racist" to include such music in my curriculum. When we talked about "black comedy," I had to preface the discussion with the fact that the word "black" had other meanings than the color of someone's skin, that it had to do with an actual color, or the color of the night sky, or the absence of light within a cave, or in literature, a mood!

Another girl got upset during an improvisation activity when a boy did a humorous rendition of a Girl Scout selling cookies because she was a Girl Scout and resented his interpretation. During Christmas time, another girl claimed she didn't want to watch "A Christmas Story" because she was Jewish. Another was upset when she saw "Mr. Bean" in a bathing suit because it violated her religious beliefs. Two boys didn't want to watch him because they claimed to do so was also against their religion. A student in an auditioned choir class told the teacher that she couldn't sing the American national anthem at school events, a part of the class curriculum, because of her Scottish heritage.

When we played warm-up games at the beginning of drama classes, students wanted everything to be "fair." They couldn't handle the spontaneity of the games in which sometimes one is chosen, sometimes one wins, and sometimes one loses. Such issues defeated the purpose of the games which was to get kids in touch with their spontaneous selves and the unpredictability of life. Kids constantly tattled on each other, especially if they didn't like the way someone looked at them, spoke to them, or acted in class. They had been conditioned in narcissistic and entitlement thinking and had learned, not only to censor themselves, but also others if something offended them.

In fact, we are allowing children to get swept up in this pervasive censoring of others. In 2007, California science teacher, James Corbett, was sued by a former student because the student was offended by Corbett's comment in class that creationism was "superstitious nonsense." In 2009, a judge found Corbett's statement to be an "improper disapproval of religion in violation of the Establishment Clause" and therefore a violation of the student's rights because the statement was "unconstitutional."[16]

The important issue raised by this case is the effect it has on educators in the classroom.   Schools are filled with students from all walks of life and from a variety of backgrounds, so someone is likely to offend another in some way.   Must teachers deliver antiseptic lessons by not talking about controversial issues?   A teacher may avoid saying something controversial about evolution because it offends a student who believes in creationism, but offends another student who does believe in evolution and wants to sue the teacher for not "imparting the facts."   Does an earth science teacher avoid informing a class that fossil records show evolution across billions of years because a creationist student objects?   Does an astronomy teacher avoid explaining that the universe began 13.7 billion years ago in the Big Bang because such an idea contradicts a student's religious beliefs?   Teachers inevitably find themselves in an absurd "Catch 22" situation because of students' rights and self-referencing behavior.

A poignant example is of a teacher who told me that after the 2012 presidential elections a student asked her who she voted for. She told the student and said nothing more.   The next day, a different student's mother, whose daughter was in the class and overheard the comment, came to see the teacher to tell her how "traumatized" her daughter was from having heard who the teacher said she had voted for.   The teacher couldn't believe it.   She explained that she did not initiate the conversation or engage the student in a discussion about politics, but merely answered the question.   She further stated that as an adult she believed that she should be direct and honest with students if they ask her a direct question because modeling such behavior is important.   What a ridiculous situation for a teacher to have to deal with when there are more important educational matters that should take up a teacher's precious time.

Hypersensitivity towards others is graduating from high school with students and accompanying them to college.   College campuses are experiencing a student movement to cleanse campuses of words, ideas, and subjects that might cause discomfort or give offense.   In fact, this climate of censorship is gradually being institutionalized on campuses.

Microaggressions and *trigger warnings* are the terms students use to identify offensive actions or words.   A *microaggression*, for example, would be to ask an Asian American or Latino American, "Where were you born?"   Such a question is interpreted as a kind of violence because it implies the person is not a real American. Another example is of a professor who, after correcting students' essays, told them that the word *indigenous* shouldn't be capitalized. Students accused him of "marginalizing" them—forget the fact he was teaching proper grammar usage. *Trigger warnings* are alerts that professors are asked to give students about subject matter that might "trigger" emotional trauma. A law professor teaching rape law was confronted by students for using the words "*rape*" and "*violence*" because of potential trauma these words might trigger. She couldn't imagine how she could teach rape law without using these words.[17]

Any emotionally-charged subject matter is susceptible to the censorship knife, including racial, physical, domestic or emotional abuse, sex, pregnancy, addiction, bullying, suicide, sizeism, ableism, and homophobia.[18] Such censorship presumes fragility of the collegiate psyche with the purpose of protecting students from psychological harm and punishing anyone who interferes with this aim—even accidentally. The danger to scholarship and quality American universities is significant. More importantly, are we creating more mentally ill people incapable of coping with diversity and unpredictability in life? In 2013, the American College Counseling Association reported an increase in the number of students experiencing severe psychological problems. A 2014 survey by the American College Health Association also found that 54% of college students surveyed said they had felt overwhelming anxiety in the past twelve months, up from 49% five-years-ago.[19] Are we becoming a society of the walking wounded? Bending the world to accommodate personal anxieties doesn't help to overcome them.

In many ways, classroom content might clash with individual views. Nevertheless, our education system must be based on inquiry and exploration. Fear of lawsuits cannot dictate the nature of education. Education should challenge students with new ideas and viewpoints. It should challenge them to examine their own assumptions because such an approach is beneficial to the mind, not a cause for legal action. Thankfully, the Ninth Circuit Court of Appeals overturned the decision against Corbett on August 19, 2011.[20]

I was incredulous at what was happening in the American classroom because I hadn't experienced such censorship in Australia. I began to monitor my own speech and behavior, censoring myself because I was unsure of what I could and couldn't talk about in class, unsure of what we could and couldn't explore in class. Several boys came up with a humorous scene for a script in which two Mexicans are trying to cross the border into the U.S. I thought their idea was clever. It showed they were aware of the issues going on within the U.S. and revealed their sense of humor. However, because of political correctness, I was unsure about letting them do the scene. I felt exasperated because humor is a healthy part of life, giving it balance; and it most certainly is an important part of the world of drama and theater. Stereotypes are often a basis of humor and teach us how to laugh at ourselves and at life and to not take everything personally. I realized that education was in danger of becoming less about challenging students than about being "appropriate" and "inoffensive." That is not to say that racist or sexist comments should be condoned, because they shouldn't, but the pendulum has swung too far in an unhealthy direction of censorship. Scrutinizing and then taking personally what other people have said has, sadly, become a cultural norm.

In Australia, I taught many of the books on the 1965-1980 list of most controversial books that were often under the censorship knife in the U.S. In English classes, we explored controversial issues related to the books. In drama classes, we performed "social drama" about teenagers and crime, drugs, alcohol, or other issues pertinent to their lives. Parents often came up to me after such performances and said how all students and parents should see the performances because of the way they explored these issues.

The Adventures of Huckleberry Finn wasn't seen as racist. No one discussed changing the word "nigger" because the book was discussed in its historical context. Twain exposed the hypocritical and demeaning way African Americans were treated in the U.S. Censorship of the book, by making it "inoffensive" or "politically correct," would not allow students to experience what African Americans went through at the time or learn to empathize with what "nigger Jim" endured. I remember my Junior English teacher, Doug Tureck, dramatically reading the scene where Huck tricks Jim into thinking he has fallen off the raft and drowned. Jim is beside himself with grief, but his grief turns to anger when he realizes Huck has tricked him:

Jim looked at the trash, and then looked at me,
and back at the trash again. He had got the dream
fixed so strong in his head that he couldn't seem
to shake it loose and get the facts back into its
place again right away. But when he did get the
thing straightened around he looked at me steady
without ever smiling and says:

What do dey stan' for? I's gwyne to tell you. When I
got all wore out wid work, en wid de callin for you,
en went to sleep, my heart was mos' broke bekase
you wuz los,' en I didn't k'yer no' mo' what become
er me en de raf'. En when I wake up en fine you
back ag'in, all safe en soun', de tears come, en I could
'a' got down on my knees en kiss yo' foot, I's so
thankful. En all you wuz thinkin' 'bout wuz how you
could make a fool uv ole Jim wid a lie. Dat truck
dah is trash; en trash is what people is dat puts dirt
on de head er dey fren's en makes 'em ashamed.

Then he got up slow and walked to the wigwam, and
went in there without saying anything but that. But
that was enough. It made me feel so mean I could
almost kissed *his* foot to get him to take it back.
It was fifteen minutes before I could work myself
up and go and humble myself to a nigger but I done
it, and I warn't ever sorry for it afterward, neither.
I didn't do him no more mean tricks, and I wouldn't
done that one if I'd 'a' knowed it would make him
feel that way.[21] (p. 85-86).

Tears welled in my eyes as I listened because it taught me about
trust, love, friendship, and the effects of betrayal that transcend social
stereotypes, race, and religious or economic differences. It taught me
what good literature does, if students are allowed to read it—
uncensored.

I also remember a hauntingly beautiful short story that I read in
middle school and that I read to my students in Australia. It would
probably be censored now in some U.S. schools because of its

"emotionally charged" content and because it doesn't paint a "politically correct" picture of a boy's relationship with his "intellectually challenged" brother. It depicts a raw and real picture of such a situation.

In "The Scarlet Ibis," a boy was embarrassed by his younger brother, Doodle, who was "intellectually challenged." Although the boy loved his brother and wanted to protect him, he also experienced anger at having to look after Doodle all the time; embarrassment at having an "imperfect" brother; helplessness at not being able to rescue Doodle; impatience because Doodle couldn't do what other kids could do; and guilt because Doodle trusted him so much.[19]

The boy decides to teach Doodle to walk and do other physical activities so that he won't be "different" from other kids when he starts school. In the process, he pushes Doodle, who doesn't complain, too hard. One afternoon, as they are rowing a boat on a lake, it begins to rain. They must quickly row ashore and run for shelter. A streak of cruelty overtakes the boy, and he runs on ahead, leaving Doodle trailing behind. When the storm subsides, the boy goes back to find Doodle, who has had a heart attack, dead under a nightshade bush. The anguish and helplessness the boy feels is irreconcilable, and he must live the rest of his life with the pain of his actions.[22]

The power of this story lies in its "politically incorrect" rawness and realness about life; no "politically" or "fundamentally" correct way exists that a person must feel in such situations. Humans often feel contradictory feelings. We need to be teaching students that human thoughts and emotions are complex and need to be explored in depth. Good literature teaches kids to do so and should not be censored. Every time I taught "The Scarlet Ibis" I had students wanting their own copies of the story because it spoke to them.

If we want citizens who have the ability to think critically and diversely about issues, we need to have an education system that values true critical thinking rather than tiptoeing around uncomfortable or controversial ideas. Rather than simply blaming teachers for students' inability to think deeply and divergently and for their diminishing levels of literacy in reading and writing, let's address the issues of "political correctness" and censorship as major contributors to the problem.

Chapter Six
No Child Left Behind
"Policy Plumbers to the Rescue"

"It's medication time," the morning mantra that Big Nurse bellowed daily at her patients in the asylum in the film, *One Flew Over the Cuckoo's Nest*,[1] ran through my mind at my school's first staff meeting for the 2011-12 school year. Her patronizing voice reverberated in my brain. An administrator was informing us of the latest state-mandated policy concerning students and medication. No one in a school was allowed to give students medication unless that person had been trained. Staff members taking students on fieldtrips must take a trained medication specialist with them if they have students who take medications—aspirins included. Said staff members must pay for substitutes out of their subject budgets to fill in for the medication specialist, or they could take a professional development class and earn credit for learning to administer medications.

I thought to myself, "Forget fieldtrips." In my thirty-eight years of teaching, students had managed to be responsible for taking their medications. Considering our litigious society, I wondered if a parent somewhere had sued a district for negligence because a child had forgotten to take his medication—to the child's detriment—and now districts around the nation were trying to protect themselves from future litigation. This issue was another example of how adults were overprotecting children. It is understandable that young children need adults to oversee the taking of medications, but to mandate such a policy for teenagers is not empowering them to become self-directed.

As I have said in a previous chapter, the entitlement mentality that grew out of the 1960s gave birth to special interest groups demanding their "rights" by pushing for government policies that would legally ensure them these rights and protection. So, mirroring American society, schools have mandated policies to regulate every conceivable interaction or situation—imagined or real—within a school. Policies governed by precise rules, regulations, and procedures, predetermine how individuals will relate to each other or must respond to each other in given situations in an attempt to "head off any problems at the pass." There are policies for classroom instruction, test taking, attendance, child abuse, sexual harassment, racial discrimination, bullying, safety, classroom management, movie watching, and protection of the handicapped. Don't get me wrong. Of course, it is important to have guidelines, policies, and procedures to run schools or there would be complete chaos. However, it is the overly-prescriptive nature of these policies that is the problem.

A demonstration of the absurdity of our policy-driven education happened to me during the 2011-12 school year. One morning an all-too mischievous boy said that his leg was hurting and that he wanted to go to the office. I didn't believe that anything was wrong with his leg, but because of children's rights and child abuse policies, I knew that I had to send him to the office. So, several minutes before I dismissed the rest of the class, I had two boys walk him to the office. A few minutes later the attendance clerk phoned me, asking if I had told the boys to carry the student to the office. I couldn't believe that she could ask such a dumb question, but I replied, "Of course I didn't, but school policy doesn't allow me to leave students in my classroom unsupervised, so I could not also supervise the boys walking down the hall to the office. Besides, boys will be boys." She told me to call her to come down to my room with a wheelchair the next time a student needed medical attention.

Several months later, I was supervising students putting stage platforms into a storage closet. One of the platforms accidently fell, striking a girl's hand before landing on another girl's foot. Remembering what the attendance clerk had said, I sent several students to the office to get the clerk to bring a wheelchair. The students returned and said that the clerk had said she was busy and that I needed to bring the girls to the office. Dilemma! I knew that it was "illegal" for me to leave the rest of my class unsupervised, but the two hurt students needed immediate assistance, so I made the executive decision to walk them to the office and hurry back to supervise the rest of the class.

I then decided that it was too dangerous for the students to put away the platforms, so we returned to my classroom. A student who stayed in the office with the hurt students returned with incident reports for me to fill out, saying that the attendance clerk needed them immediately because she couldn't attend to the students until she got the reports. I quickly filled them out and sent the student back to the office with them. I immediately received a curt phone call from the attendance clerk chastising me for sending private information down to the office with a student because I was breaching the student privacy policy.

I couldn't believe it! Exasperated, I reiterated that I was not allowed to leave my class unsupervised, and since she couldn't treat the students without the reports, I sent them down to the office in the timeliest way possible. She then asked me why I hadn't called her when the accident happened; to which I replied, "I was in a storage room without a telephone." Since the auditorium next to the storage room had a telephone, she asked me why I hadn't sent a student to call from there. More frustrated than ever, I said that we teachers had been adamantly instructed by her office never to allow students to use any school phones other than the main office phone from which she was calling, and I would be breaching that policy if I had allowed a student to use the auditorium telephone. I well and truly understood Joseph Heller's message in his novel *Catch-22*.

A former teacher now working at Star Bucks said that she could no longer stand all the policies. She felt as though she were in a straitjacket, being scrutinized, and then criticized if she made a policy or procedural mistake. Another teacher, who had been teaching for only two years, said that she had a sinking feeling when she went to work each day because she was afraid she would make a mistake and get in trouble for not precisely following policies. She also felt discouraged at the lack of open or honest communication among staff members and administration at her school. It was as if everyone followed an "education-speak" formula based on being "politically correct" with the fear of litigation looming in the air. Phillip Howard expressed the feeling:

> A paranoid silence has settled over the workplace. Only a fool says what he really believes. It is too easy to be misunderstood or to have your words taken out of context. . .The absence of spontaneous give-and-take stifles the dream of mutual understanding just as it diminishes enjoyment. . .And, rather than uniting us in the workplace or as a country, we have disintegrated into a country of factions with each group preoccupied with its entitlements—at everyone else's expense.[2] (p. 135-137).

Our drive for certainty and perfection has left nothing to chance, and people are no longer allowed to use their internal compasses or common sense to guide them when it comes to determining what is right or wrong, to figure out how to solve a problem, or to make decisions at their places of employment. Policymaking requires making decisions that affect people's lives without their having a chance to cast a vote. According to Diane Ravitch, (who has been an education policymaker), to think like a policymaker means to look at schools, teachers, and students from an altitude of twenty thousand feet and to see them as objects to be moved around by big ideas and great plans with no practical understanding of their effects within the classroom.[3] Consequently, we have created a society and school environments where behavior and relationships are prescriptive, lacking in spontaneity.

Many teachers feel that they have become disenfranchised in their profession; they are little more than hamstrung classroom technicians expected to deliver mandated education policies. They no longer have autonomy in their classrooms; they are no longer able to use their professional training, skills, and judgment to develop curriculum and teaching strategies. Experienced teachers, who would go beyond the clichés in their choices of what and how to teach, are no longer allowed to do so. Creativity and innovation are deadened by the uniformity of educational publishing and testing.[4]

No policy has affected American education as much as the signature No Child Left Behind policy instituted by the Bush administration in 2001. No Child Left Behind—a policy based on faulty assumptions—was doomed to failure because of its "politically correct" concerns and its unrealistic expectations of students, teachers, and school districts. My first contact with No Child Left Behind was on August 28, 2002, the first day of school at a small rural high school in southern Colorado where I would be teaching freshman and sophomore English, speech, and drama classes. When the principal began discussing the expectations and implications of No Child Left Behind, my common sense made me think, "This sounds idealistic and unrealistic." We all get "left behind" at various times in life because we don't all have the same aptitudes, talents, or even interests in succeeding at the same things. I wondered if the policy would expect unrealistic results from students, giving them unrealistic expectations about what they could and couldn't achieve. I wondered if it would lead to feelings of inadequacy in some students, frustration in others, and an inability to accept individual strengths and limitations in still others.

I well remember taking geometry in high school. I hated it. It bored me. I couldn't understand why we had to prove a "triangle was a triangle." It looked like one to me. The arts were my forte. My geometry teacher warned me that I would be in deep trouble by the end of the year if I didn't memorize the theorems early on in the course. She was right. While other students were solving geometry problems, I was rifling through the text trying to find theorems to solve the problems. I received a "D." I didn't protest the "D," ask my parents to intervene on my behalf, or threaten the teacher. I deserved the grade I received. What I learned was that my interest did not lie in the field of mathematics. It wouldn't have made any difference if the teacher had let me use my "learning style" to do geometry. Writing a poem about theorems or dramatizing a triangle didn't interest me. No one tried to intervene to help me to get a higher grade, and the teacher wasn't blamed. The fact was: I was "left behind in geometry." And, as Ned Kelly, the notorious Australian outlaw, once said, "Such is life." We all have our limitations and our weaknesses, and it is a relief to know what they are so we can then focus on our strengths and interests.

The principal at my new school went on to talk about the importance of the CSAP tests, how they were related to NCLB, and how the results would affect the school's funding and its end-of-the-year report card which, in turn, affected whether students "choiced into or out of" the school.

I wondered: Since when did a school receive a report card? Since when did students/parents have a choice as to where students went to school? Was it really true that a school could be punished and face sanctions if it didn't "make the grade"? Did she really mean that a school could be closed if it wasn't showing growth and improvement in test scores? Since when did test data and enrollment statistics become the barometer of what students have learned? Could a public school really lose federal funding if it continued to have poor results? Why weren't the many variables that determined student success or failure in school taken into account? I wondered what teachers really thought about such a policy.

The principal stated that freshman and sophomore English classes would be part of the CSAP testing that year. Although I had taught college prep English in Australia, which focused on preparing students to take college entrance exams, I wasn't sure if I knew enough about the American system to take on the challenge of preparing students for the CSAP test. My fears were unfounded when my freshman and sophomore English classes jumped 20% points in both reading and writing on the CSAP test that year, and the school was noted in a state newspaper for its gains in reading and writing. Still, I jumped at the offer of a drama teaching job at another school, in another city, for the next school year. I didn't want to submit myself professionally to what I perceived was happening in education due to NCLB.

NCLB had changed the American government's role in education. The operation and oversight of public schools in the United States was typically the responsibility of states and local communities. Throughout the nation's history, the federal government was not expected to play a major role in regulating or directly financing schools. This law changed that idea. The quality of education became solely dependent upon standardized test scores. The rise and fall of test scores would be the variable for judging students, teachers, principals, and schools.[5] And, sadly, Bush and Paige's policy would also set the tone for a punitive approach to education.

The focus of the NCLB Act is threefold: 1. Increased accountability through testing and teacher certification; 2. Greater school choice for students through vouchers; and 3. More flexibility for state and local education agencies to spend money as they see fit as long as Annual Yearly Progress (AYP) is attained. The law emphasizes the content areas of math, reading, writing, and science. Social studies, arts, humanities, and technology are glaringly absent.[6]

Nationwide Accountability Systems

- School districts nationwide must create accountability systems that cover all schools and students.
- Accountability will include testing for all students in grades three to eight.
- These accountability systems must be based on state standards in reading and mathematics.
- Accountability will include annual statewide progress objectives that ensure that all groups of students reach "proficiency."[7]

Annual Yearly Progress

- Failure to meet adequate yearly progress (AYP) toward statewide proficiency goals will subject schools to improvement procedures, corrective action, and restructuring measures.
- Schools that meet or exceed AYP objectives or close achievement gaps will receive State Academic Achievement Awards.[8]

School Choice for Parents and Students

- School districts are required to spend up to 20% of their Title I allocations to provide school choice and supplemental educational services to eligible students.
- Schools that persistently fail to meet state standards for at least three of the four preceding years must allow low income students to use Title I funds to obtain supplemental educational services from public- or private-sector providers.
- Local Educational agencies (LEAs) must give students attending schools identified for improvement or correction the opportunity to attend a public school designated as

"better," including public charter schools within the school district.

- The school district must provide transportation to the new school and must use at least 5% of its Title I funds for the purpose, if needed.
- Choice and supplemental service requirements are intended as an incentive for low-performing schools to improve if they want to avoid losing students along with the portion of their annual budget associated with these students.[9]

Although the NCLB Act retains the Elementary and Secondary Education Act's (ESEA) emphasis on improving the academic performances of disadvantaged students, it adds significant accountability requirements for all schools and school districts that receive federal funds.[10]

The Act had already required that states define standards and develop assessments in the above mentioned subject areas; NCLB turned them into a nationwide high-stakes accountability system with punitive sanctions attached. Sanctions are a fact of life and they make sense in many respects. For instance, students should lose points when they don't do homework and employees should be docked pay if they don't come to work. However, NCLB didn't take into account many factors such as differences among students and student populations, differences in base knowledge and skill levels of students; the characteristics and stability of students' home lives, economic status, and physical and emotional health; safety issues in and out of school; access to appropriate class materials and school funding from state to state; language barriers; and the ways that students learn. Rather, every school was tarred with the same NCLB brush and held accountable in the same way. It was assumed that students led standardized lives and were thus suited to taking standardized tests.

Not only do NCLB's underlying accountability assumptions appear to be invalid, but more critically, not enough fiscal, human, and social resources exist to create fifty state systems of education that ensure 95% of students pass one high-stakes test. *Accountability* was the sound-bite of public officials and business leaders in the 1990s who wanted measurable results in education so they would know that tax dollars invested in public education were getting a good return. Predictably, that is what NCLB blindly sought.[11]

The policy's main assumption, that "high stakes" tests could identify with certainty which students should be held back, which teachers and principals should be fired or rewarded, and which schools should be closed, was flawed in another way.[12] Standardized tests are not precise instruments because, like all tests, they have a margin of error and the same student could produce different scores on the same test on different days. Testing experts have warned that these scores should not be used in isolation to make major decisions about the success of students and schools.[13] Moreover, psychometricians claim that year to year changes in test scores for individuals or classes may be due to random variation; and tests may be invalid if too much time is spent preparing students to take them—a situation that has become the rule rather than the exception in many schools. Still, none of these points is taken into account when determining a school's success and teachers' accountability.[14]

Establishing Annual Yearly Progress (AYP) may not only be an assessment fallacy but a misapplication of ordinary business principles.[15] Humans are organic beings, not inanimate numbers and statistics. Individuals grow at different rates and times, and no one can force anyone to fit a mathematical, statistical "banking recipe" for growth. Also, as shown above, variables outside of the classroom, both genetic and environmental, determine a student's growth. We can't force plants, trees, and flowers to grow; and neither can we force children to grow. We can nurture and guide their growth; but we can't force them to grow to suit predetermined, statistical benchmarks.

Besides, how can teachers be held accountable for whether or not specific students reach the AYP benchmark when many teachers don't have the same students from one year to the next or from one quarter or semester to the next, depending on subject and school? One can possibly measure the growth of students at the beginning of a school year and then at the end of that same school year in a specific subject with a given teacher, but one can't compare growth from one year to the next with different classes and/or different teachers. For example, if a middle school teacher teaches sixth grade math it is highly unlikely that the same teacher will have the same students the following year because the students will have a different teacher who teaches seventh grade math. Since no two teachers have the same teaching styles and techniques, you can't accurately calculate students' AYP in relation to specific teachers' performances, which the NCLB policy has tried to do.

Because the arts' subjects in my school district don't have standardized tests by which to demonstrate AYP, the district decided to implement common assessment tasks for each subject area within the arts. The battle began when we middle school drama teachers met with administrators from the district office. We tried to explain that we had no valid way to statistically compare students' growth from year to year or within the same year because our classes were only a quarter long, and we did not have the same students from quarter to quarter or from year to year. The only way to evaluate growth was to give students in a class a common assessment task at the beginning of the quarter, then, administer the same task to the same students in the same class at the end of the quarter.

Even more absurd is the fact that severe needs' students are required to take modified state standardized tests in reading, writing, math, and science, despite the fact that many of them can't read, let alone comprehend the tests. Many of them can't even communicate. But, schools are mandated to give all students "equal" opportunities. A designated paraprofessional must sit with each student and ask the student each question and when he/she doesn't respond, the paraprofessional notes "no response" next to each question. Tax payers are footing the bill for this method, and schools reap the consequences because these students' scores lower the overall scores of the schools, affecting their yearly report cards, and possibly leading to punitive sanctions for schools and individual teachers.

For three years, I had a severe needs' boy in my drama class who was in a wheel chair and couldn't move or speak. He was expected to participate in the drama common assessment task because the law mandates that all students must be treated equally. The year that we piloted the task, I graded him "not proficient" because he couldn't participate. When I submitted my results, I asterisked his name and noted that he was "not proficient" because of his special circumstances. When the data sheet for the district's middle school drama classes was published, it didn't identify this student as having special needs that wouldn't allow him to complete the task. Thus, if my "accountability" came into question, it would appear that I wasn't competent in helping the said student achieve AYP in drama. Situations such as these frustrate teachers, especially since talk of "merit pay" and of firing "incompetent" teachers has come into play. More importantly, is this approach to education—which paints all students with the same brush—really concerned with the true welfare or ability of a student with the type of severe needs that this student had?

NCLB's destructive core sets schools up for failure because test scores do not necessarily indicate real progress when they rise or deterioration when they fall. Many of the tests used to judge our students, teachers, and schools are "norm-referenced;" which means they are specifically designed to ensure a certain proportion of "failures." In addition, errors in question design, scoring, and reporting have always been a part of standardized testing and are likely to increase substantially with the increase in mandated testing.[16] Also, many states have found ways to pretend that they have met the impossible goal. Because the law allows states to develop their own standards, choose their own tests, and define proficiency in their own way, most states have reported progress every year. Some states began to set lower standards in order to meet the law's requirements, so much so, that what constituted "proficiency" varied across the country, making the law and its requirements a farce. For example, Mississippi reported that 89% of its fourth graders were at or above proficiency in reading, but according to NAEP, only 18% were proficient.[17] According to a study entitled, "The Proficiency Illusion:"

> The testing enterprise is unbelievably slipshod. It's not just that results vary, but that they vary almost randomly, erratically, from place to place and grade to grade and year to year in ways that have little or nothing to do with true differences in pupil achievement. . .The testing infrastructure on which so many school reform efforts rest, and in which so much confidence has been vested, is unreliable—at best.[18] (p. 3).

Despite these drawbacks and discrepancies, "punitive" sanctions have been meted out to schools that did not reach NCLB bench marks.[19]   The following "corrective measures" may be taken if a school "flunks" the AYP benchmark five years in a row:

- The school staff may be replaced.
- New curricula may be instituted, with appropriate professional development for the staff.
- The school's administration may be given significantly decreased management authority.
- An outside expert may be appointed to advise the school.
- The school day and school year may be extended.
- The school's internal organizational structure may be revamped.[20]

If the above-mentioned schools still do not improve, further measures might be taken:

- Students may be transferred to another public school.
- Supplemental education services may be continued.
- The school may be closed and then reopened as a charter school.
- All the school staff, which includes the principal, may be replaced.
- The school district may enter into a contract with a private management company, with a demonstrated record of effectiveness, to operate the public school.[21]

One teacher described the nightmare she and her colleagues endured when her school was placed on an improvement plan for not demonstrating AYP. The rural school's population comprised students who lived permanently in the town, transient students whose parents were either in the military or were migrant, seasonal workers, and students who were designated special or severe needs. The students who lived permanently in the town always demonstrated AYP, but the transient and special/severe needs' students did not. The "improvement plan" expected teachers to follow prescribed, scripted curricula which meant that they had to deliver the lessons verbatim off the scripts to ensure that all students received the same instruction. A "pacing calendar" outlined the amount of time teachers spent on each lesson before they had to deliver the next lesson. The role of the principal and other administrators was to monitor classrooms to ensure teachers were delivering lessons with fidelity. If students didn't understand math, reading, or language arts' concepts teachers were not allowed to use their own professional judgment to reteach the concepts. This "improvement plan" was designed by authorities outside of the district and was then imposed on the district with no consideration of its cultural, social, or educational contexts.

The teacher pondered the future of her school. She couldn't imagine it would ever make AYP because of its transient and special/severe needs' population. The next phase of sanctions would include firing teachers and administrators. She couldn't foresee new teachers or administrators wanting to work at the school because of the rigid, punitive, and unrealistic expectations NCLB had placed on the school.

Accountability and its punitive sanctions have led many desperate teachers, administrators, schools, and districts to find ways to beat the system as indicated earlier in this chapter. Charter schools have cheated almost four times the rate of traditional public schools.[22] Ways to get high test scores include:

- Restrict admission of low performing students.
- Reduce participation by encouraging low performing students to stay home on the day of the state test.
- Expand the pool of test takers who are eligible for accommodations so that this boosts a school's "proficiency" numbers.
- Engage students in saturation of test preparation.
- Change student answers.
- Change scores.[23]

New York papers have accused New York of using "Enron accounting" when reporting test scores and dropouts. Massachusetts' claim of a 93% statewide graduation rate in 2004 was challenged by data that demonstrated that only 71% of the kids that started ninth grade actually graduated. Illinois school superintendent

Robert Schiller revealed that schools are pressured into pushing out truant or low-performing students in order to meet the requirements for improving test scores. The growing number of dropouts in Chicago—up to 17,400 in the 2001-2002 school year—is indicative of the use of this strategy.[24]

Fear of not making the grade and of being threatened by sanctions has also led to schools narrowing students' education experience. When Garfield/Franklin elementary school in Muscatine, Iowa, was threatened with NCLB sanctions, the school's response was to no longer do eagle watch on the Mississippi River or go on field trips to the University of Iowa's Museum of Natural History. Creative writing, social studies, and computer work became occasional indulgences.[25]

The Center on Education Policy surveyed a nationally representative group of schools in 2007 and found that 62% had increased time spent on reading and mathematics in elementary schools while 44% said that they had reduced time spent on science, social studies, and the arts so that more time could be spent on test preparation.[26] A further frustration is that students at risk of not doing well on the mandated tests are often taken out of arts' subjects and placed in study skills and success-maker classes to help them improve in the academic areas being tested on the state standardized tests. This approach undermines the integrity of these subjects and takes away an important area of learning and development for students. A balanced curriculum should be the focus of a well-rounded education system and well-rounded students.

Schools increasingly expect teachers to take prescribed professional development classes that focus on how to improve test scores in the subject areas being tested. Also, some schools expect teachers of subjects such as band, choir, drama, art, and physical education, as well as the reading teachers, to teach reading skills,— even if doing so does not fit in with the syllabi they have designed for their classes.

Schools have also resorted to forms of bribery to get kids to do well on tests. In Racine, Wisconsin, schools have given out movie passes or entered students in drawings for shirts, other personal items, and even televisions and DVD players.[27] Such desperate measures speak volumes about the fear, stress, and frustration educators, administrators, and school districts face on a daily basis in

their attempt to ward off sanctions that could lead to job loss and the closing down of schools. Due process has been totally ignored by NCLB.[28] The Fifth Amendment to the U.S. Constitution states:

> No person shall be held to answer for a capital, or otherwise infamous crime, unless on a presentment or indictment of a grand jury, except in cases arising in the land or naval forces, or in the militia, when in actual service in time of war or public danger; nor shall any person be subject for the same offense to be twice put in jeopardy of life or limb; nor shall be compelled in any criminal case to be a witness against himself, nor be deprived of life, liberty, or property, without due process of law; nor shall private property be taken for public use, without just compensation.[29]

NCLB has held schools accountable for the same so-called "crimes of failure" each year. Double jeopardy doesn't apply. It would be a sad state of affairs if schools and/or school districts had to begin using the U. S. Constitution to regain the power that NCLB has taken away.

Over the decade, more and more criticism of the NCLB Act has surfaced in scholarly journals, the media, and educational communities. A prominent criticism is that school districts, administrators, and teachers are caught up in an educational paradigm not of their own making. The system is a "top down," policy-driven system of policymakers, many of whom have probably never been in the classroom, making educational decisions—a practice antithetical to the highly respected Finnish school system. For example, President Bush appointed Margaret Spellings as U.S. Secretary of Education; she has a bachelor's degree in political science; she never taught or worked in a public school, nor had she had experience running a large, complex organization.[30] Many educators feel like "cogs in the machine of education." They have never been asked to state their beliefs on education or to even reflect on what they believe. They are expected to implement what the "experts" decide is best policy.[31]

Education Nation on msnbc.com recently reported that classrooms are in crisis because many of today's teachers have minimal to no classroom experience. Once again, a situation unlike that of the successful Finnish model in which teachers are recruited from master's degree programs with the promise of high pay and professional autonomy. The decline in experienced teachers in the classroom has increased dramatically. In 1987-88, the median teacher had fourteen years' experience. By 2007-08, the median had dropped to eleven. The national commission on teaching estimated that three hundred thousand veteran teachers retired between the years 2004-2008. The decline is attributed to numerous factors such as widespread retirement of Baby Boomer teachers, unrealistic demands due to the NCLB policy, and to teachers leaving to find better-paying jobs in other fields. Also, nearly 50% of new teachers leave the profession within their first five years. Complaints most commonly mentioned by teachers include: inadequate working conditions, more rigorous testing, larger classes due to budget cuts, time scarcity, the requirements of NCLB, and isolation from other teachers and staff. [32]

NCLB is based on the false assumption that poor teaching is the primary cause of unsatisfactory student performance. Teachers facing pressures to perform, often resort to teaching to the test to protect themselves from the threats and sanctions they may face if their students do not perform well. Further frustration stems from the fact that they realize that punitive actions fail to address the underlying problem of poverty and inadequate school funding, which are major reasons that many students start off behind and never catch up. [33] Large class sizes, inadequate books/resources, outmoded technology, and high student mobility also impede improvements in teaching and learning, but are being ignored. [34] Again, issues that are dealt with in Finland by universal adequate funding and regulated class sizes.

Focus on test scores creates pressure on children; even though any testing is generally stressful at all age levels, when test results are widely publicized in local newspapers and television, the trauma skyrockets. [35] Education researchers Mabry and Margolis (2006) report that in a study they conducted, many teachers claimed that their students experienced test anxiety and that their efforts to minimize their students' anxieties were largely futile. These teachers worried about the impact of "high-stakes" test-taking on their students' self-esteem, motivation, and aspirations. [36]

Children usually think that adults are all-knowing and all-wise and that they often feel that they have to produce or else. The students who fail to achieve may feel they are letting down their teachers, the school, and their parents, and this is a heavy burden for children to bear.[37]

When teachers and administrators see that student test scores are read as a measure of *their* competence, they often concentrate on how well students do on tests rather than on how well students learn. Children are thus given the message that passing tests rather than meaningful learning is what is important in school. As one observant seventh-grade Kentucky student explained, "The test is taking away the real meaning of school. Instead of learning new things and getting tools for life, the mission of schools is becoming to do well on the test."[38]

Finally, one of the most profound effects NCLB has had on students is what it teaches them about life and work. When schools focus on end results or grades rather than on what the grade is supposed to mean as achievement, it is not any wonder that when young people go out into the work world, they are often less concerned with the work than with the pay for the job. If young people are treated as products, worth only as much as they score on a test, then they need have no other moral or ethical scruples than any other industrial product would have.[39]

Rosanna Pittella's book, *How Deconstructing the American School System Will Reconstruct the American Dream,* analyzes the NCLB policy, stating that only lip service was given to the testimony given by educators, administrators, and other subject matter experts on education at the Congressional hearings that transpired before the policy's implementation. These experts warned legislators of the disastrous effects such a policy would have on the education system. Their concerns included:

- The destructive nature of overly zealous summative as opposed to formative testing.
- The correlation between socioeconomic gaps and achievement ones.
- The critical nature of early learning and school preparedness and sufficient special and bilingual-education.

- The inequity of funding to schools resulting in everything from overly large class sizes to deteriorating infrastructure and facilities to insufficient access to technology.
- The diminishing support for mental health services and counseling services in schools.
- The diminished support for instruction in music, the arts, and character learning.
- The increased red tape imposed by increased federal involvement in school administration.
- The diminishing numbers of those choosing education as a profession.[40] (p. 61).

After fourteen years of implementation, NCLB's stated goals have not been met nor do documented results appear to be tracking at the pace necessary to meet them:

> The assumptions that informed NCLB, among them, that standardized testing can act as an optimal catalyst and best measure of learning, that teachers are accountable above all others for student performance as measured by standardized tests, and that education policy can be defined and implemented successfully at the federal level...were found to be faulty.[41] (p. 193).

President Obama's education policy "Race to the Top" has added insult to injury. Like all major federal education initiatives, it was not written onto a blank slate but was shaped by the educational landscape created by the implementation of NCLB. I imagine that many educators, including myself, had hoped that President Obama would see the detrimental effects of NCLB and would dismantle the policy. However, RTTT did no such thing. Rather, the policy's catchy title implied that education was indeed a competition, a "race to the top" with money as a reward, awaiting school districts that could meet the policy's demands and "reach the top."

RTTT adopted NCLB's concept for increasing student achievement and decreasing achievement gaps among students, focusing on state and local policy developments that NCLB encouraged. Obama administration officials believed that educational success would occur if states developed overall strategies of reform and that RTTT would help develop those strategies by offering funding to states that "successfully" demonstrated their development and commitment to: a) adopting internationally benchmarked standards and assessments that prepare students for success in college and the workplace; b) building data systems that measure student success and inform teachers and principals about how they can improve their practices; c) increasing teacher effectiveness and achieving equity in teacher distribution; and d) turning around the lowest achieving schools.[42] According to President Obama:

> America will not succeed in the 21st century unless
> we do a far better job of educating our sons and
> daughters… And the race starts today. I am issuing
> a challenge to our nation's governors and school boards,
> principals and teachers, businesses and non-profits,
> parents and students: if you set and enforce rigorous
> and challenging standards and assessments; if you put
> outstanding teachers at the front of the classroom;
> if you turn around failing schools – your state can
> win a Race to the Top grant that will not only help
> students out-compete workers around the world,
> but let them fulfill their God-given potential.[43]

To administer the RTTT competition, the federal education department enlisted a group of peer reviewers to rate the states' submitted proposals. The states were primarily evaluated on their past track records of policy development and past records of student success, what the department called "state reform conditions," and on their future proposals for using the RTTT money, known as their "reform plan." The department provided the reviewers with a rubric to score the proposals, using a five-hundred-point scale. The rubric allocated points in the following seven areas, which were further broken down into more specific criteria: state success factors (125 points); standards and assessments (70 points); data systems to support instruction (47 points); great teachers and leaders (138 points); turning around the lowest achieving schools (50 points); other general areas (55 points); and the extent to which state applications made teaching of science, technology, engineering, and mathematics a priority (15 points). Multiple reviewers examined each proposal.[44]

The twenty-first century education arena is reminiscent of the farcical antics played out in the 2001 movie, *Rat Race*.[45] In the movie, Donald Sinclair, an eccentric owner of the Venetian Resort Hotel Casino in Las Vegas, challenges six casino patrons to a no-holds barred race from Las Vegas to Silver City, New Mexico, to retrieve two million dollars in cash hidden in a duffel bag in a train station locker in Silver City. The cross country caper begins after the patrons are given keys to the locker and are sent on their way. The patrons become embroiled in a variety of hilarious predicaments as they revert to underhanded tactics to get to Silver City first. The viewer is taken on an outlandish adventure in which nothing goes according to plan.

A "rat race" is defined as an endless, self-defeating or pointless pursuit such as that of a lab rat trying to escape while running around a maze or in a wheel. It is also defined as expending a lot of effort running around, but ultimately achieving nothing meaningful. It is easy to see a parallel between the movie and American education policy.

Predictably, as educators, students, and schools nationwide have spent years enforcing the NCLB and RTTT mandates in education, the pendulum is swinging in a semi-new direction. On December 10, 2015, the federal government signed into law the Every Student Succeeds Act (ESSA). Replacing the NCLB Act, the law gives states more flexibility and control, but maintains the corporate mindset of NCLB with its focus on standards, testing, and accountability as keys to student success. States will be given leeway in how/when they test students, in whether or not they adopt Common Core Standards, in what accountability goals they set, and in how they evaluate teachers, but they must submit accountability plans to the federal Department of Education. However, federal punishment for schools, principals, and teachers whose students have low test scores and Annual Yearly Progress will end.[46] In essence, with the inception of ESSA, states will merely be left to their own devices to continue administering NCLB's failed measures. Only time will tell how these changes playout. And, the proverbial rat race of corporate education reform continues in its modified form.

American education has reached a critical point. If it is to be truly concerned about each student's education, educators, researchers, and policy makers must find a way to move forward. The Zen story about the empty cup states what initially needs to be done:

> A well-known professor went to visit a Zen master.
> As the master gracefully served tea, the professor
> described his ideas of Zen. The master remained
> quiet as the professor spoke, continuing to pour.
> When the tea reached the brim of the cup, the Zen
> master kept pouring. The tea overflowed, spilling
> onto the tray, the table, and the carpet, until the
> professor could no longer stand it. "Stop!" he said.
> "Can't you see the cup is full?" "This is you," said
> the master, positing to the cup. "How can I show
> you Zen, until you first empty your cup?" [47]

Assessments and data have largely driven education, while the ability to think creatively has been "left behind." Because "what is measured is treasured," the liberal arts curriculum, so long cherished in the United States, may be in jeopardy of being "left behind." Educators who hold a more humanistic, holistic view of the purpose of education are frustrated because the meaning they assign to education differs greatly from the meaning assigned by society or their schools.

The focus of education needs to shift from mirroring our consumer, product-oriented society to that of questioning the fundamental assumptions and definitions presidents, politicians, policymakers, and profiteers hold about education. Philosopher Krishnamurti believed that education should prepare students to understand the whole process of life rather than merely equip them to pass examinations and get jobs.

To Krishnamurti, the true function of education should be to cultivate the intelligence to try to find answers to life and its problems. It should motivate individuals to find out for themselves what is real, and what is true, without a formula. [48] We need to stop the rat race, quit churning out a society of test takers, and foster a society of blossoming Krishnamurtis.

Chapter Seven
No Corporation Left Behind
"The Customer is Always Right"

Two thousand people rallied in Lower Manhattan on Sept 17, 2011. Inspired by protests and uprisings across the Arab world and by feelings of frustration and helplessness, these protesters comprised a leaderless resistance movement of individuals from all walks of American life. October 17, 2011, a month after its inception, people from around the world joined the cause. Karanja Gacuca, a former Wall Street analyst, articulated the concerns of many when she stated:

> I am here to celebrate the 30th day of this protest
> against corporate power. Concerned about the
> egregious Wall Street bonuses—particularly after the
> industry accepted a tax-payer bailout and the middle
> class continues to be squeezed—I believe it's time
> for a fairer system that provides health care, education,
> and opportunity for all, and rejects corporate influence
> over government.[1] (p. 1).

The corporate image brings to mind savings and loan scandals, corporate bailouts, outsourcing of jobs to other countries, downsizing and hostile takeovers, inflated bonuses for corporate executives, tax loopholes and failure to pay corporate taxes, and, ultimately, a focus on greed and profit-making as the main goals in life. The self-interested, self-seeking corporate mentality has gained a stranglehold over the global community. It's no wonder why so many people around the world are voicing their concerns about where life on planet earth is headed if we allow corporations to continue to run roughshod over us.

The Raiding

I was introduced to "corporate education" in 1986. I took a year's leave of absence from my teaching job in Australia to return to Colorado to spend time with my ailing father. Before visiting with my father, I decided to stop in Carson City, Nevada, to visit Richard, the husband of my mother's best friend who had recently died.

Richard mentioned a business endeavor he and his business partner were initiating and inquired about my interest in becoming involved because of my teaching background. The men had an idea for a "profit-making" summer program for high school students to take place in the grandeur of Sion, Switzerland, a ski resort. Enticing as the plan sounded, I hesitated because I had never viewed education as a "profit-making" venture. But Richard was persuasive, and I'd always been a risk-taker with a love of new adventures. So, my involvement with corporate education began.

I became the director of "Swiss Connection Summer Program." Though we developed a business plan together, I found the experience surreal. Problems developed because Richard had an entrepreneurial, corporate mentality based on the importance of the logical, the rational, and the profitable. My focus was more on the mystical, the unpredictable, the intuitive, and the educational. Even so, we decided to spend the rest of 1986 developing and marketing the program with the idea of offering our first sessions during the summer of 1987. He projected that we would have two summer sessions with at least fifty students in each session.

When he began talking about shareholders, profits, dividends, and a return on his investment the first year, I began to waver. I told him that education wasn't a product but a process, so it was highly unlikely that we would make enormous profits. He insisted that he had calculated it on paper and that was all that was needed to be successful. So I stayed with the project.

As I traveled around the country attending summer camp expos, other camp directors told me that we were unlikely to get one hundred students the first year. They had started their programs with five to six students the first year, building their programs and reputations from there. The process was gradual, they said, which is what I had sensed from the start.

I told Richard what I had learned, and his response was to question whether I was trying hard enough to sell the program. I felt he was focusing on me as the problem—similar to the current attitude that ignores the dynamics in the classroom and primarily blames teachers for students' lack of academic success.

In the end, we did get six students who wanted to attend. However, because our "business plan" wasn't designed for a small group of students, we were unable to start during the summer of 1987. Richard lost his commitment to the program and withdrew his money. He ended up with a tax deduction while I came away with an experience in expressing my creativity. But, I also grew even more wary of the idea of mixing corporate and educational philosophies.

Until the late 1970s, corporations had minimal influence on public education. But, as the toy industry grew in the twentieth century, corporations started to focus on the money that could be made by tapping into the children's market.[2] A "merchandise frenzy" developed after Walt Disney linked toys to his film *Snow White and the Seven Dwarfs* in 1937. The marketing techniques used to promote adult consumerism began to cultivate consumerism in children. In the world of toys, children were saturated in an "ethos of fantasy consumerism."[3]

In fact, twenty-first century American culture has become so commercialized that, according to education professor Henry Giroux, corporations hustle children on all fronts and have transformed childhood into a market strategy.[4] American companies spend fifteen billion dollars each year marketing to children under the age of twelve. In turn, parents, influenced by their children's demands, spend about five hundred billion dollars a year on toys, junk food, and other consumer products for their children.[5]

Moreover, TV is no longer the sole advertising agent for children. Video games, the Internet, cell phones, iPods, and schools have also become vehicles for advertisers to reach children. According to Benjamin Barber, author of the book *More Democracy! More Revolution*:

> It is time to recognize that the true tutors of our
> children are not school teachers or university

professors but filmmakers, advertising executives, and pop culture purveyors. Disney does more than Duke, Spielberg outweighs Stanford, MTV trumps MIT.[6] (p. 15).

The Exploitation

Because schools across the nation are facing budget crises, many have become desperate to find other sources of funding. Corporate partnerships are attractive for this reason. Many schools have unquestioningly become fertile ground for sowing the seeds of consumerism within children, teaching them that consuming goods is the essence of a person's identity and of the good life. The bottom line for kids is that:

> They are being subjected to marketing messages in school—some hidden, some obvious, but all quite powerful. The place where they might be learning how to deal with commercial pressure is thrusting more commercial pressure on them.[7] (p. 70).

Channel One, a marketing company news broadcast, is a prime example of corporate intrusion into schools and children's minds. The channel broadcasts ten minutes of news to eight million children in twelve thousand schools across the U.S. with two minutes of commercials. The former president of Channel One, Joel Babbit, states that "the biggest selling point to advertisers lies in forcing kids to watch two minutes of commercials."[8] Another company, Zap Me, offers schools free equipment such as computers and Internet browsers in exchange for being able to advertise online and collect data on what children are interested in to give to advertisers and marketers.[9] Carolyn Vander Schee, a doctoral student at Georgia State University, whose research focuses on health and educational policy, observes:

> The public school represents one of the last frontiers not already dominated by market segmentation, market penetration, and corporate profits. At the same time, the public school also represents one of the most, if not the most, strategically focused,

captive, and lucrative markets in American society.
It is no wonder that corporate America has invaded
this new territory of impressionable consumers,
a territory that provides access to the demographic
segment with the greatest buying power.[10] (p. 1).

Randy Hewitt, who teaches a graduate course in the history and philosophy of American education, says that the commercialization of public schools concerns him as a parent, "especially the unquestioned faith in corporate-school partnerships."[11] He believes that schools are becoming permeated with corporate advertising and commercialism. Such advertising teaches students that the essence of the "good life" lies in "selling and consuming candy, wrapping paper, stationery, Christmas candles, and various other overpriced trinket items."[12]

His concern arose while witnessing a corporate-sponsored fund-raiser at his daughter's middle school. The fund-raiser was designed to inveigle middle schoolers to sell consumer goods to help make money for their school. The marketing spiel at his daughter's school began thus:

By a show of hands, how many of you like candy,
you know, World's Finest Milk Chocolate with
almonds or the delicious Mint Meltaways that
everybody knows and loves? Many of you have
raised your hands. This is absolutely great...How
many of you like cars, especially limousines with
lunch in the back with your favorite person? Now,
some of you aren't raising your hands. But I know
something that absolutely everybody wants and that's
money: cold, hard cash...If you want to be a part
of something exciting and good, if you want to help
your school and community, then stand up and show
that you are willing to take part in this wonderful
opportunity. Come on, stand up! Some of you aren't
standing. Look around at your friends. Come on,
get them on their feet and make them a part of this
fantastic opportunity.[13] (p. 47).

What an amazing use of manipulation to get pre-teens to "do the right thing" according to the world of consumerism. What better way to lure teenagers than by appealing to their emotions? Appealing to their sense of guilt, their need to be part of a peer group, their fear of being "left behind," their need to feel important, and their sense of duty to "do the right thing." The appeal to guilt is one emotional technique, among many others, that I strove to make students aware of in my English classes. I hoped to make them discerning adults in this pervasive world of consumerism.

At the 2011 Education Nation conference held at Rockefeller Center in New York City, many schools reported that they had begun displaying corporate advertising on the sides of school buses, on students' lockers, and at sporting events. The advertising generated sorely needed money for educational and extracurricular activities whose budgets had been cut due to the nation's economic slump.[14] The practice is understandable, but it is a sad comment about the state of the American education system.

Giroux observes that advocates of corporate culture and corporate partnerships have lost sight of public education's civic function, which is to educate citizens capable of participating in a democratic society whose values include justice, respect for children, and rights of citizens.[15]

The Farming

One of the most harmful ways that corporate partnerships are infiltrating schools is via school cafeterias. According to Eric Schlosser, author of *Fast Food Nation*:

> Not satisfied with marketing to children through
> playgrounds, toys, cartoons, movies, videos, charities,
> and amusement parks, through contests, sweepstakes,
> games, and clubs, via television, radio, magazines,
> and the Internet, fast food chains are now gaining
> access to the last advertising-free post of the American
> life: the public school.[16] (p. 51).

More than 20% of schools now offer brand-name foods in their cafeterias. Major fast-food chains, such as McDonald's, Subway, Papa John's Pizza, Dunkin Donuts, Pizza Hut, Domino's Pizza, Taco Bell, and Dairy Queen, provide about 73% of fast foods within schools.[17] Soft drink vending machines are prevalent in almost 50% of all school districts.[18] Schools cut deals with soda and snack vending companies to increase discretionary funds for optional programs and to strengthen core academic curricula. A school in Beltsville, MD made $72,438.53 in the 1999-2000 school year through partnership with a soft drink company.[19]

Allowing fast-food giants into school cafeterias compromises school lunch programs. Nutrition experts emphasize the importance of establishing healthy eating patterns in childhood because nutrition affects children's health, their ability to learn, and their potential for becoming healthy adults. Studies have shown that a diet high in junk food affects children's behavior, cognition, and focus.[20] According to a 2009 study published in the "European Journal of Clinical Nutrition," children whose diet is high in junk food are more likely to be hyperactive than those whose isn't. Hyperactivity results in a lack of focus and concentration, affecting students' cognition in the classroom. Fatigue may also result from a sugar crash because junk food is high in fat, sugar, and calories and is lacking in the essential nutrients needed to balance blood sugar levels. School lunches provide about one-third of children's daily caloric intake (potato chips or French fries make up about one third of American children's vegetable servings).[21]

Over the past three decades, weight problems and obesity have increased in children and adolescents. The obesity rate in twelve to nineteen year olds in 1970 was 5%. This figure doubled by the 1990s and exceeded 15% by 2000.[22] Although there is no solid evidence to support their suspicions, policymakers are concerned that increased availability of junk food in schools contributes to the growth in childhood obesity. This also means a rise in immediate and long-term health risks such as asthma, osteoporosis, tooth decay, Type 2 diabetes, hypertension, and cardiovascular diseases. Also of concern is the decline in physical education and recess in many schools. These schools have felt the need to spend more time on academic subjects because of accountability measures requiring students to achieve on standardized tests. Such schools feel the need to overcompensate, lest they suffer the consequences from lack of such achievement.[23]

On July 20, 2006, Children Now, a non-profit research and advocacy organization, hosted "The Future of Children's Media: Advertising" conference in Washington D. C. Keynote speaker Senator Hillary Clinton expressed her concern about the childhood obesity epidemic and urged companies to temper their advertising of junk food to kids. Other speakers at the conference also voiced concern. However, politicians and health experts voicing such concerns does not guarantee that they will be heard by corporations bent on making profits and on denying the negative effects of junk food on health. It's difficult to pass legislation to restrict the advertising and sale of junk food in schools. Advocates report that congressional leaders tend to favor corporate interests over the health and well-being of kids. Election laws allow corporations to donate money to legislators' campaigns, and they do so as long as the legislators support their pro-corporation agenda:[24]

> In 1970, Americans spent about $6 billion on fast food; in 2001, they spent more than $110 billion. Americans now spend more money on fast food than on higher education, personal computer software, or new cars.[25] (p. 11).

So, when policymakers blame teachers for America's poor performance in the global arena, they need to look at factors such as junk food's effect on children's abilities to learn. Fortunately, the "October as National Farm-to-School Month" resolution, which passed in the House of Representatives on November 17, 2010, offers hope on the political horizon. Sponsored by Representative Holt of New Jersey, the resolution's goals are not only to foster local farm job growth and to stimulate local economic development, but also to ensure American children receive quality food at school. The resolution reinforces the commitment of the House Committee on Education to improve how food is sourced for school lunch programs in an effort to fight childhood obesity.[26]

Schools across the country participate in National Farm-to-School Month. Manitou Springs, Colorado, organized a local food discussion evening in celebration of this special month. Community members were able to chat with others about local food in schools and community farming. They were also able to hear about The

Galileo School's Greenhouse Project in which students participate in growing the school's food. First-graders at R.B. Hunt Elementary School in St. Augustine, Florida, celebrated the month with a visit from USDA's Dr. Janey Thornton, chef David Bearl, a chef involved in the Chefs Move to Schools program, and a local farmer. Students learned about food harvesting and production and about making healthy food choices to maintain a healthy lifestyle. Growing awareness and community involvement may help to counteract the damage done by corporate fast-food partnerships in schools.[27]

It may also take individuals such as reality TV chef and food activist Jamie Oliver with his "Food Revolution" to impact school lunch programs. He transformed the British school food program. Now his goal is to replace processed and junk food with freshly cooked meals in schools across the U.S. He states that he has been overwhelmed by the thousands of people who have voiced their concern about the quality of food being served at schools. He emphasizes that "the sodas, chocolate milks, and pizzas children are eating for breakfast, lunch, and dinner are putting them at risk of developing problems that often go hand-in-hand with a diet of poor quality, cheap food: obesity, diabetes, behavioral problems, and poor school grades."[28]

The Controlling

Corporate intrusion into education is more detrimental than marketing unhealthy food. In 2009, the Koch brothers funded a group called Americans for Prosperity (AFP), which financially backed school board candidates, advocating the end of mandated busing in Wake County (Raleigh), North Carolina. The candidates won, took over, ended the busing, and effectively re-segregated the classrooms.[29]

The Koch brothers and AFP have also contributed large amounts of money to other candidates running for school board elections throughout the country in an attempt to stack school boards with conservative members who will do their "corporate bidding." This bidding includes turning public education into a privatized, free-market enterprise, disempowering teachers' unions, encouraging neighborhood elementary schools to compete with one another, directing tax money to pay for religious education, and creating a pay scale that pays teachers according to their subject areas.[30]

In fact, the Koch brothers and AFP were successful in buying control of Douglas County School District in Colorado where they claimed they would spend more than $350,000 on the school board campaign. Their candidates won the election, and Douglas County is now viewed as a model for transforming public education along corporate lines across the country. The new conservative board launched the first voucher program in the U.S. to subsidize private and parochial tuition for wealthy families in the district. These schools, which include those that have a Bible-based, creationist curriculum, have received a down payment of funds—but the program is on hold, pending court challenges. The district has also added more charter schools and given funds to subsidize books/classes for home schooling.[31]

Many parents and teachers within Douglas county are aware that the board has been bought, and they see the board's reforms as splintering the community. So, to counter the influence of the bought board, they have established their own groups, launched Facebook pages and websites, organized protests, filed complaints and lawsuits, and made open-record requests in an attempt to scrutinize board members and make them accountable for their actions. Then, in November 2015, voters in Douglas county overwhelmingly chose to recall three school board members who were part of the corporate reform agenda's attempt to gain a stranglehold of the district. Voters gave a clear message that they want their public schools to be based on a community-oriented model of education rather than a corporate-dictated one that has a hidden agenda of privatizing the public school system by dismantling it and replacing it with for-profit charter schools.

However, AFP is increasingly investing in local elections, including statehouse races in Arkansas and Kansas, judicial races in Florida and North Carolina, and mayoral races in Lakeville, Minnesota and Coralville, Iowa. One of AFP's goals is to undermine public education in favor of charter schools and vouchers. This can be accomplished by backing candidates/politicians who will do AFP's bidding.[32]

Additionally, by offering strings-attached grants to institutions of higher learning such as Florida State, AFP can set up departments, create programs, and control hiring to regulate the message they want delivered in the classroom.[33]

The disturbing trend in schools is the transformation from public institutions, influenced by community collaboration based on democratic ideology, to that of profit-making, entrepreneurial entities based on free-market ideology.[34] Besides being infiltrated by corporate-based partnerships, schools are being modeled after and structured along corporate guidelines. "Corporate education," conjures up images of stakeholders, customers, clients, business plans, high-stakes testing, charter schools, vouchers, choice, school-business partnerships, merit pay, accountability, CEO-type management, performance-based outcomes, and product-based education rather than process-based education.

Since 1980, business leaders have embraced the report "A Nation at Risk's" claim that American schools are falling behind and should be modeled after corporations.[35] Education is no longer about teaching and learning. Its purpose is to prepare a workforce that will ensure that the U.S. maintains its consumer-oriented way of life. Economic interests overshadow democratic ideals and practices that involve the development of critically thinking, responsible, and community-minded citizens who understand the importance of ethics and integrity in life.[36]

Many schools, in corporate fashion, have mission statements—often "proudly displayed in school lobbies, in teacher handbooks, in school improvement plans, and even in various school-to-home correspondences."[37] The main goal of these statements is to establish the climate and direction of an institution, along with its purposes and values. However, according to Donna Breault, assistant professor of educational leadership at Georgia State University, often an institution's written mission statement is at odds with its pursuits. Many schools relate their mission statements to ideals of democracy and citizenship, yet the consumption ethic that has infiltrated schools undermines these ideals and what it means to be a critically thinking and critically aware citizen. Breault emphasizes for example that:

> Rather than focusing on a common good defined
> in terms of collaboration or sharing, many of the
> fund-raising activities encourage competition among
> students. The market mind-set focuses on

self-interest rather than the egalitarian practices of citizenship.[38] (p. 63).

The market-mindset often cancels out or confuses the issue of educating students to critically participate in a democratic society. We need to be reminding ourselves and cautioning students about the true nature of our school system. We need to say something similar to that of the quote from Doris Lessing's novel *The Golden Notebook*, which I presented to my English students at the beginning of a school year:

> The child is taught that he is free, a democrat,
> with a free will and a free mind, lives in a free country,
> makes his own decisions. At the same time he is
> a prisoner of the assumptions and dogmas of his time,
> which he does not question, because he has never
> been told they exist. He does not know that he is
> already moulded by a system. . .Ideally, what should
> be said to every child, repeatedly, throughout his
> or her school life is something like this: 'You are in the
> process of being indoctrinated. We have not yet
> evolved a system of education that is not a system of
> indoctrination. We are sorry, but it is the best we can
> do. What you are being taught here is an amalgam of
> current prejudices and the choices of this particular
> culture.'[39] (p. xv-xvii).

Beyond the problem of mission statements is the reality that NCLB, which has been the foundation for education over the past fourteen years, is a business plan. Its emphasis is on core market concepts such as standards and accountability, competition, rewards, sanctions, and consumer choice. In a free-market economy, education has become a consumer good, knowledge has become a commodity rather than an intrinsic state of mind, and students have become the products we manufacture on the assembly line of education. Schools and classrooms are marketplaces and the business rhetoric of efficiency and performance are the bottom line goals of the system.[40]

When schools are run as businesses within an education "marketplace," serious problems can develop because of the inherent conflicts between market places and "educational environments." Market places sell "products" to customers/clients and are underpinned by competition from competitors who offer similar products. In order to stay in the competition, the vendors must continually solicit customers/clients, often operating from the premise that the "customer is always right." Accommodating and pleasing customers becomes a major goal to avoid losing them to the competition. Such an approach works in places like Walmart and Target because they are selling inanimate objects that can't think, speak, or act. Such stores do not "make" these products. They merely sell them. Schools, by contrast, nurture human beings with their unique genetic makeup and their unique and unpredictable thoughts, emotions, and behavior. Such an endeavor involves the complexity of human interaction and the development of relationships. Human beings are organic and active/re-active not inanimate objects to be bartered.

For the past fourteen years, parents, students, local communities, and the nation have been led to believe that the success of a school hinges on the simplistic view that what constitutes and defines "getting an education" relies on results from state standardized tests and on school report cards that prescribe annual growth. And, if a school doesn't "make the grade," punitive actions will solve any problems. Notwithstanding, we have become a nation based on entitlement, self-advocacy, and "helicopter parenting," which can compromise a school's effectiveness.

Because school funding is based on student numbers, many schools allow themselves to be "hijacked" into doing whatever they have to, to maintain student numbers, taking a "customer is always right" approach to dealing with students and parents. In earlier chapters, I discussed at length how an entitlement, self-advocacy approach, taken to the extreme, can keep students (and their parents) in narcissistic frames of reference where they are absorbed in placating their own wants, needs, and perceptions, regardless of teachers' professional opinions or recommendations or the ultimate educational or developmental benefits to students.

A case in point is an email from a parent to a counselor that was sent to me by mistake. An angry parent chastised the school and threatened to send his son to another school because the son wasn't improving in math. The father claimed that the boy was participating in homework club after school, was attending an after- school math class, and was enrolled in a study skills class during the day, yet his son's grades weren't improving. He stated that any "reasonable" person would conclude that the boy's failure was the fault of the school. My conclusion was that any "reasonable" person would deduce that after receiving so much extra help, maybe the boy didn't have the aptitude for math. Blaming teachers and the school wasn't going to change that fact. However, because parents have been trained to scapegoat teachers and to see schools as businesses and themselves as either satisfied or unsatisfied customers, he felt justified in his accusations. (The parent had seemingly been conditioned to believe the unrealistic edict that "no child will be left behind," regardless of ability, motivation, or genetic and/or environmental factors.)

Another example is that of a substitute teacher who was taken aback when she mistakenly received a voicemail on her home phone from a parent who thought that she was leaving a message for her son's teacher. The message stated that the parent was upset because her son had received a "D" in the class and that her family did not accept "D" grades. She, therefore, expected the teacher to give her son either an alternative assignment or an assignment for extra credit that would change the grade. Once again, the "customer is always right" attitude is alive and well within some communities of parents.

The market-oriented education system reinforces the "instant gratification" *modus operandi* in life. Instant gratification is a reiteration of the "terrible-two's" tantrum throwing. Nurturing and guiding toddlers through this phase of development requires setting boundaries. People must accept delayed gratification. They must learn that commitment, hard-work, self-discipline, patience, time, and even sacrifice are the necessary steps in gaining what they want in life.

According to psychologist M. Scott Peck, life is difficult and confronts us with a series of problems that we must learn to deal with and to solve in order to give our lives meaning. Peck believes that confronting and solving problems is a lifelong process that calls forth our courage and wisdom, allowing us mental and spiritual growth. He states that discipline is the basic tool needed to solve problems; delayed gratification is an important component of learning to exercise discipline.[41]

A classic study in delayed gratification was conducted in 1972 by psychologist Walter Mischel of Stanford University at Stanford's Bing Nursery. Over a six year period, he offered over five hundred children, ages four to six, a marshmallow each, promising them two instead of one, if they could resist eating the first marshmallow. Scientists analyzed how long each child resisted the temptation to eat the marshmallow and whether or not doing so affected their future success. The analysis showed a strong correlation between children's being able to resist eating the first marshmallow and their achievements later on at school (and even their weight!). Following the same subjects at ten-year intervals, Mishel's study found that those children who were able to delay gratification were less likely to drop out of college, use cocaine, or end up in prison.[42]

Most endeavors in life require discipline and delayed gratification. Men and women in competitive sports exercise discipline when practicing their sports, delaying gratification until game day. Artists, musicians, actors, and writers embrace the artistic process which utilizes discipline and delayed gratification in order for them to master their particular artistic endeavors; skilled workers such as plumbers, electricians, and surveyors exercise discipline and delayed gratification to learn their trades, reaping the rewards when they can finally practice the skills they have mastered. Academics embrace the discipline process and delayed gratification in order to become qualified in their areas of expertise.

For students, discipline and delayed gratification in their studies and their activities will lay a foundation for their pursuits as adults. School is a training ground. When a school allows students to opt out of situations they find disagreeable because the school feels threatened, the school is unintentionally letting these students down like the parents who indulge them. Also, because commercialization and corporatization of schools has created this "clientele mentality," teachers have little say professionally about what transpires in the classroom. Their professionalism is compromised.

The Organization

Keeping with the corporate theme, some school districts now

hire CEO's from the corporate world or individuals from military backgrounds to serve as principals and superintendents who must diligently implement NCLB. Such individuals usually have had little to no experience in education or as teachers working with students in the classroom. According to freelance journalist and international educator, Heather Wokusch:

> A pumped-up corporate definition of intelligence
> is making headway in US society. CEOs are
> regarded as experts on political and sociological
> change, and excellence in public education is
> defined in terms of its service to the private sector.
> Equating intelligence with conformity to corporate
> values is not a new concept, but the extent to which
> wisdom is being confused with business expediency
> is an increasingly insidious trend.[43]

An article in *The New York Times* titled, "Applying Corporate Touch to a Troubled School System," focuses on New York City's Yonkers school district's superintendent, Andre J. Hornsby, who has been deemed a model for the current concept of leadership in urban schools. The *Times* described him as "arrogant, autocratic, an egomaniac…adamant that poor minority children can overcome their socioeconomic hurdles, driven to raise scores on standardized tests using cookie-cutter curriculums, and assuming an almost militaristic take-charge approach."[44]

The article reveals that one of Hornsby's first initiatives was to increase teacher workloads. That gesture led not only to teachers going on strike, but also to Hornsby ultimately winning a court battle which prevented extra resources from being given to "eight school districts the courts identified as being in most need." Hornsby exemplifies corporate leadership that is autocratic, is not concerned about inequality, and is bent on reducing curricula to standards and testing—relegating teachers to having little to no say in teaching and learning.[45]

San Diego also hired a non-educator Alan Bersin as superintendent from 1998-2005, giving him *carte blanche* to reform the district's schools. The San Diego business community, along with major foundations that awarded the district millions of dollars, supported Bersin's appointment. Bersin was a former prosecutor. After consulting with education experts at Harvard University, he and his team of experts, led by Anthony Alvarado, who gained notoriety as superintendent of District 2 in New York City, set out to close the achievement gap within the San Diego school district. They were determined to bring changes to every classroom even if this meant disciplining resistant teachers and firing reluctant principals.[46]

A uniform approach to teaching reading was mandated with all principals and teachers trained in the techniques of "Balanced Literacy." Elementary teachers were required to teach reading for three hours every morning using the mandated method. Principals were required to spend at least two hours each morning visiting classrooms to make sure teachers were using the prescribed method. Bersin and Alvarado reorganized the school system and changed its culture.[47]

They were not interested in school-based decision-making, in site-based management, or in involving teachers in curriculum and instruction matters. The strategy was based on command-and-control methods rather than on consensus. In military fashion, their strategy had three axioms: "1) Do it fast, 2) Do it deep, 3) Take no prisoners." Bersin's "business plan" was called, "Blueprint for Student Success in a Standards-Based System." It emphasized the importance of uniformly training teachers who would have "the same practices, the same ideas, and the same language—which he believed would increase student achievement."[48]

Many principals and teachers were disconcerted by Bersin's approach. They felt disrespected by his lack of collaboration and consultation, claiming that reform was being done to them rather than with them. Ninety percent of the district's principals were replaced and teacher resignations and retirements doubled during Bersin's "reign of terror." More than one-third of the district's teachers left between 1998-2005. The district's student dropout rate increased every year during Bersin's tenure, growing to 23% by 2005.[49] According to Ravitch:

> Teachers, especially veterans, spoke about being
> harassed. They complained about mandates and
> directives that narrowed what they were permitted
> to teach…those who didn't go along were bullied.

Teachers were punished by grade switching: A
first-grade teacher might be reassigned on short
notice to teach sixth grade, while a sixth-grade
teacher would be reassigned to teach kindergarten
or first grade. Principals spoke in hushed voices
about the abrupt public removal in June 1999 of
fifteen administrators. The theory behind these
new tactics, several said, was "culture shock,"
keeping everyone on edge, afraid, insecure.[50] (p. 61).

Another example of a corporate style leadership is that of
Superintendent Mike Miles of Harrison School District 2 in Colorado
Springs, Colorado. Mike Miles was one of the most activist
superintendents in the nation. He is a military man who also served
as a diplomat in Moscow and Warsaw with the U.S. Department of
State at the end of the Cold War. After such a career, he decided to
turn to the "humble profession" of teaching and taught at Fountain-
Fort Carson High School for four years. He was then promoted to
principal of Fountain Middle School and eventually became assistant
superintendent of curriculum before accepting Harrison's top job. It
took him eleven years to rise from first-year teacher to
superintendent of an eleven thousand student district.[51]

Miles' focus for the 2009-10 school year was his "Effectiveness
and Results" pay-for-performance plan which would pay teachers
based on how their students performed on a variety of tests and on
how they were rated by their principals who observed them in the
classroom. Teachers who didn't meet standards would be dismissed.
Miles' approach included ordering that all classroom doors in all
schools be open at all times. He sent principals to training meetings,
then escorted them into classrooms where they were coached how to
spot good and bad teachers. He took charge of the district's
curriculum, narrowly defining what kids needed to learn and when
they needed to learn it. More instruction hours and days were added
to the school year; teachers were required to attend meetings together
to look at student performance data and to give each other advice.
And, the students began to take more tests with Miles commenting
that he saw nothing wrong with "teaching to the test" if it is a good
test.[52]

At the end of the 2010 school year, controversy erupted at a D2 school board meeting when teachers who had been evaluated "unsatisfactory" voiced their protest. A library/media specialist was dismissed because he couldn't show student achievement data proving that he was a good employee. The only data he could provide, other than his testimony, was that he raised library circulation by 88% during a time period when his school saw a boost in its state reading scores.[53]

A seventh grade science teacher provided graphs that illustrated her students' achievement was strong and that her principal's evaluations had been positive up until the time she had been removed as department chair because she forgot to turn in a paper, and she commented on her Facebook page that she could use a drink.[54]

Other teachers also presented their cases. Eventually, Miles interjected that teachers were presenting "misinformation" to the board and that he stood behind his principals' decisions.

On Thursday, September 15, 2011, one hundred and fifty students from Sierra High School protested outside of their school in support of teachers who had been let go. Several students spoke, enumerating their concerns: longer classes, shorter lunch breaks, deleted elective courses, abolition of shop and child development classes, and, most importantly, the issue of their teachers' fear that they will be fired because they can't meet standards and AYP.[55]

Critics of Miles believe that his approach will ultimately fail because it is based on fear and intimidation that will drive experienced teachers, and any teacher with an ounce of self-respect and dignity, out of the district. Moreover, Mike Stahl, leader of the Pikes Peak Education Association, observed, "When the teachers feel pressure, guess who else is going to feel pressure? The kids. Also, the system will drive out anyone who dares to show any insubordination to administration." A district employee stated:

> I'm proud to work in D2... Our kids need our
> help and support, but with Miles in charge, the
> district will struggle. There is a climate of fear in
> D2 because of the tactics that he employs. There
> are great people working in D2. People who have
> a special gift of connecting with our kids! But

unfortunately, Miles is not one of them. He leads by fear. Sadly, leading by fear only puts people in survival mode. Teachers who are working under this cloud of fear may be effective for a short time, but WILL NOT do well in the long run. I don't believe that Mike Miles knows how to, can, or is truly willing, to change the way he leads.[56]

Hornsby's, Bersin's, and Miles' approach to school management is one of "measure and punish." It has created an atmosphere at many levels within the country of "let's blame teachers" for the problems. Worse than Hornsby, Bersin, or Miles is Michelle Rhee, the former Chancellor of DC Public Schools, who is the "rock star" of corporate education reform. Her influence has reverberated across the nation, paving the way for a corporate stranglehold on education.

Rhee became a national symbol for her brash, get-tough management style. Before becoming Chancellor of DC Public Schools, as a member of Teach for America, Rhee taught for three years in a Baltimore elementary school managed by Education Alternatives Inc., a for-profit organization. According to Rhee, the proportion of her students who read on grade level during her second and third years of teaching, leapt from 13% to 90%—a questionable claim since critics have never been able to locate Baltimore records verifying this claim. Rhee, who spent only three years in the classroom, claimed that "effective" teachers could overcome poverty and other disadvantages.[57] Veteran teachers like me, who have spent many more years in the classroom, are justifiably wary of a chancellor who can make such claims, especially since most studies find that new teachers are less effective than experienced teachers and that a teacher's first two years of teaching are the least effective. But, in this world of corporate education, one doesn't have to be an educator to be a principal or a teacher. In fact, a degree in education is obsolete because the assumption is that all a teacher needs to do to be "effective" is to be a good manager. Such corporate education also presumes that a teacher is the single most important factor in student achievement.[58]

From the outset Rhee had said that "teachers are everything," yet declared public education in DC to be an entrenched, failed system with teachers to blame for its failure. In Fast Company magazine in October 2009, she stated that she laid off two hundred and sixty-six teachers in order to get rid of teachers who had hit children, had sex with children, or had missed seventy-eight days of school.[59] In fact, only one had had sex with a student and only eight others were alleged either to have used corporal punishment or to have had excessive absences. Such rhetoric influences public opinion about teachers. It eases the way for free market, corporate policies such as top-down organizational structure, privatization of schools, school choice, getting rid of teachers' unions, running schools like businesses, blaming teachers for education's failure, making educational experience optional for leadership positions in education, and measuring academic success by data.[60]

Rhee resigned as Chancellor in 2010. The aftermath of her reign has been an ongoing investigation by the Inspector General of the Department of Education as to whether Washington D.C. school officials cheated to raise test scores during Ms. Rhee's tenure.[61] Also, evidence is surfacing which indicates that during Rhee's time as Chancellor, shoddy test score data with high margins of error were used to evaluate teachers. Teachers were divided into categories of low, below average, average, above average, or high, depending on their test scores, and then compared with the scores that a "model" expected students to receive. As a result, the data showed seventy-three cases in which teachers whose students produced consistently outstanding test scores – at or above the eight-fourth percentile citywide – were nonetheless tagged as below average. The reason? The formula expected even better results, based on the demographics and past performance of the students.[62]

After resigning as Chancellor, Rhee went on in late 2010 to create StudentsFirst--an organization whose goal was to raise one billion dollars in its first year to transform public education nationwide and to become education's lobbying equivalent to the National Rifle Association. The organization's focus was on teacher quality, teacher evaluations, school accountability, and the expansion of charter schools.[63]

Luckily, Rhee recently stepped down as CEO of the organization which had a high staff turnover rate, embarrassing PR blunders, and a lack of focus. Word has it that Rhee alienated many supporters because she wasn't a team player, and they viewed her tactics as "imperious, inflexible, and often illogical."[64] So, maybe there's hope for the future in terms of "re-humanizing" the public education system. Let's hope that more parents, teachers, and administrators, who have had to work in districts with individuals such as Rhee, also get fed up with such a leadership style and either vote with their feet or work together to get rid of such leaders.

Many superintendents and principals around the country may be exasperated by the system but feel helpless to do anything about it. The likes of Hornsby, Bersin, Miles, and Rhee become newsworthy because of the controversial influence they are having on education reform. According to one NYC school teacher, who asked not to be named, "up until the last ten years, a principal was something like the conductor of an orchestra: a person who had deep experience and knowledge of the part and place of every member and every instrument."[65] However, in the past ten years, we have seen the emergence of leadership academies such as those of Mayor Mike Bloomsberg's Leadership Academy and Eli Broad's Superintendents' Academy designed to produce "cookie cutter," formulaic principals and superintendents whose approach to leadership mirrors that of corporate CEO's.

One frustrated principal, who wished to remain anonymous, stated that he recently left the education profession, after serving nineteen years as an administrator, to deliver sandwiches for a friend's catering business. He had been superintendent in four rural communities and had also been superintendent overseas for the Department of Defense where he oversaw eighty-six schools in nine countries over seven time zones. He believes that American education is creating a "work force" rather than creating free thinkers and entrepreneurs. He defined "education" as complying with policies and procedures; following timelines and schedules; and proving that you have "educated" students. A major reason he left education was because he was tired of constantly having to deal with entitled parents' and students' demands. He believes that parents and students run schools and that such a situation has compromised administrators and teachers because their professional judgment has become irrelevant.

Corporate education has created a division of "bad administrator vs. effective administrator" and "bad teacher vs. effective teacher." Factors such as over-demanding or unsupportive parents, poverty, malnutrition, lack of student motivation, and aptitude are all deemed excuses of the "bad administrator or teacher" that can be overcome by the "effective administrator or teacher." During the 2011-2012 school year, my colleagues and I were introduced to the "effective teacher" when we were required to read a book for our all-school professional development course that gave bullet point ideas about what makes an "effective" teacher.

When I read the book, my immediate thought was, "How glib, trite, and dangerous this book is with its simplified recipe for what makes an effective teacher." I wondered who and what qualified the author to write about what constitutes being an "effective teacher." Other colleagues agreed. One teacher checked the author's credentials and couldn't find any information about how long he had been a teacher in the classroom before becoming a principal. Another said that she wondered if his motive was to get onto the bandwagon of blaming teachers for the dysfunctional system because of the money to be made on the lecture circuit. A novice teacher was upset by his focus on teachers as the key to success in the classroom—ignoring all the factors that gag teachers.

To me, the book presented bullet-point findings in a presumptuous fashion, and findings were supported with questionable examples such as the claim that at school assemblies the "ineffective" teachers lean up against the wall, whereas the "effective" teachers sit with the students. Such statements are simplistic, cosmetic observations of what constitutes being an effective teacher.

In the current educational climate, books such as this, which give bullet-point answers to what makes teachers effective, could have an unrealistic effect by suggesting a "magic formula" for what a teacher must do to ensure that students statistically demonstrate growth. Since states must come up with their own educator accountability schemes to determine whether a teacher is worth keeping or paying more, it is all too easy to develop "tick-the-box" measures based on such books.

One of Obama's criteria for winning Race to the Top money was for states to adopt a numbers-based teacher evaluation system keyed to standardized tests. Colorado was the first state to implement new teacher evaluation laws in 2013, mandating that 51% of yearly evaluations must come from students' test score gains.[66]

Administrators face the same scrutiny and evaluation process, thus consolidating an educational environment of formulaic teaching and learning. Predictably, I recently received an email offer titled "Seeking Talented Trainers! Wanting to earn one thousand dollars and much more per day training teachers?" The promo states:

> We are a national staff development company and
> we train in PK – 12 grade schools nationwide
> (public/private and charter schools). Our trainers
> are compensated based on the materials the school
> purchases. The more participants attending the
> training and/or materials the school purchases…the
> more you earn each training day…Our best presenters
> have a business mindset![67]

This seems to me that another company is trying to profit from the move toward corporate education. Will such "teacher training" courses cause college and university teacher education courses, designed and taught by educators, to become diminished or obsolete? And, how will such courses frame and/or taint the meaning of what it is to be a teacher? Only time will tell. Teachers are not clones, and we need more than expedient,"tick the box" technicians in our classrooms. As William Deresiewicz states in his book *Excellent Sheep: The Miseducationof the American Elite and the Way to a Meaningful Life:*

> Teaching is not an engineering problem. It isn't a
> question of transferring a certain quantity of infor-
> mation from one brain to another…A teacher's job
> is to lead forth the powers that lie asleep within her
> students. A teacher awakens, a teacher inspires…A
> teacher is a midwife, Socrates said. If you are
> "pregnant in soul," he says in Plato's *Symposium,* your
> teacher's presence makes you team with thoughts
> that beg to be released into the world…a teacher
> helps you to discover things inside you that you
> didn't know were there.[68] (p. 174).

Behind the scenes, education is also being undermined by powerful private foundations and their corporate heads. Diane Ravitch refers to them as members of the "Billionaire Boys' Club"[69] while Henry Giroux refers to them as "hedge fund reformers, billionaire industrialists, and corporate vultures."[70] Well-known entrepreneurs such as Bill Gates, Eli and Edythe Broad, the Walton family of Walmart fame, and the aforementioned Koch brothers, have established foundations whose sole motives are to reform American education:

> The "reform" movement is really a "corporate reform" movement, funded to a large degree by major foundations, Wall Street hedge fund managers, entrepreneurs, and the U.S. Department of Education. The movement is determined to cut costs and maximize competition among schools and teachers. It seeks to eliminate the geographically based system of public education as we have known it for the past 150 years and replace it with a competitive market-based system of school choice— one that includes traditional public schools, privately managed charter schools, religious schools, voucher schools, for-profit schools, virtual schools, and for-profit vendors of instruction.[71] (p. 19-20).

Foundations have always gifted money to educational organizations. But earlier foundations such as those of Ford, Rockefeller, and Carnegie allowed these organizations the autonomy to do as they thought best with the funds.[72] However, the key players today take a "venture philanthropy" approach, seeing their monetary gifts as an investment from which they expect a personal "return." Consequently, they define what they want accomplished, how they want it accomplished, and then decide who will accomplish it. These foundations fully support the corporate reform agenda: money and power influence the outcomes desired, mirroring their philosophies of unfettered competition, deregulation, incentives, and other market-based approaches. Such an approach is contradictory to the world of education where value should be placed on collaboration.[73] One of the benefits Gates, Walton, and Broad receive is that they

> gain huge tax write-offs from the money they invest in schools. They use these tax deductions to save money, while the taxpaying public loses valuable tax revenue and cedes control of publicly funded schools to rich and powerful corporate moguls. In reality this scenario isn't philanthropic at all. It is morally and politically irresponsible because it represents a form of hostile generosity that serves to expand the power of the corporate rich over public schools while offering the illusion that they are enriching public life.[74] (p. 18).

So, their excessive wealth and power influence policies as it allows them to circulate and promote their market-driven values and disdain for public education via the media. The documentary film, *Waiting for Superman,* for example, was promoted in *New York* magazine and the *New York Times* and on the *Oprah Winfrey Show. Time* magazine is planning a conference focusing on the reform strategies endorsed by the film. CBS Evening News also presented a series of segments from the movie.[75]

In essence, the film promotes charter schools, corporate values, market-driven reforms, and a military style of leadership. It claims to present a balanced commentary on the state of public education when, in fact, it doesn't. It targets public education, teachers, and teachers' unions. It makes no mention of the problems that exist within charter schools such as the corruption and cheating of school administrators, the dismissal of underperforming students, or the refusal to accept students for whom English is a second language, or students who have learning disabilities. Public schools and teachers are demonized in the film, and no mention is made of any of the extensive studies that have found that fewer than seventeen percent of charter schools outperform public schools.[76]

And, more importantly, thirty-three states permit charter schools to be operated by for-profit organizations and to be paid for with taxpayer dollars. "Even in states that don't allow for-profit schools, like Ohio, charter schools are allowed to contract out their management and/or services to for-profit operators, and often the boards of the charters are financially entangled with the operators who make a profit."[77] For example, Arizona state law doesn't prohibit a charter from doing business with board and/or staff members:

> In 1998, Michael and Olga Block founded Arizona's
> Basis charter schools….In 2009, the Blocks established
> a for-profit corporation to supply the six Basis charters
> with "most everything they need to operate: school
> directors, teachers, accounting, technology, human
> resources, public relations and Michael and Olga Block."
> The non-profit corporation signed a ten-year agreement
> with the for-profit. Michael remained on the board
> of the nonprofit, while Olga resigned. According
> to *The Arizona Republic,* "The nonprofit paid the Blocks'
> company $9.8 million out of $13.7 million in total
> spending." Under state law, the state may audit the
> charter school but not the for-profit corporation hired
> to run the school.[78]

Needless-to-say, the FBI is investigating the operation and the financial records of many charter schools across the country.

Charter schools are not the only alternatives to public education that are being promoted by free market, school choice advocates who buy into the corporate reform movement's agenda that our public school system is failing and that alternatives to public education are the antidote to improving the nation's achievement gap and low scores on international tests.   Virtual and blended schools are increasing across the nation despite persistent poor academic outcomes and little knowledge about their internal workings, according to a new analysis from the National Education Policy Center.

> In 2013-14, 262,000 students in 33 states were enrolled
> in 447 full-time virtual schools that deliver all instruction
> online, according to the NEPC. Another 26,155 students
> across 16 states were enrolled in 87 blended schools,
> which combine traditional face-to-face and online
> instruction. Despite rising enrollment numbers, however,

these virtual and blended schools fared poorly when
compared to traditional public schools on a host of
academic measures, according to the new study, titled
Virtual Schools Report 2016: Directory and Performance Review.
One glaring example: The 4-year graduation rate in
2014-15 was 40.6 percent for full-time virtual schools
and 37.4 percent for blended schools, compared to 81
percent for the nation as a whole.[79]

The report also states that virtual and blended schools have struggled to make yearly progress in the three states that still use "adequate yearly progress" to measure school accountability. And, in states that have replaced AYP with other systems for rating school performance, only 30.6% of virtual schools were rated "acceptable" in 2014-15. The percentage was worse among virtual schools run by EMOs. Also, 82% of the 121 virtual schools for which data were available, had lower proficiency rates on state math and English/language arts exams than state averages. Seventy-seven percent of independently managed blended schools also scored below state averages.[80]

Because corporate culture permeates American society, it is inevitable that many Americans give unquestioning allegiance to this corporate norm and believe whatever films such as *"Waiting for Superman"* want them to believe about the American education system. A friend, who has known me since I began teaching thirty-eight years ago and has always been aware of my passion and commitment to education, said that he didn't claim to know the dynamics of what was going on within education reform. However, from the information he gleaned via the media, from hearing about *"Waiting for Superman,"* and from listening to Michelle Rhee on the news, he could see we'd gotten a handle on the problem. I realized that he, like so many others who aren't directly involved in education, was developing a different picture of what is going on within education from that of what educators are experiencing. That is why it is so important for educators, parents, students, and communities to find their own voices and speak up before it's too late.

In order for a society to survive, it is important for it to have a strong sense of community; to be not only concerned with the needs of individuals but also with the needs of the society as a whole. By instinct, humans are social animals, and from tribal times, have lived in groups for the survival and good of everyone concerned. Membership within a community teaches people values intrinsic to human relationships: a sense of security, of belonging, and of protection; the importance of cooperation, camaraderie, compromise, and commitment; a sense of responsibility towards, and respect for, others within the community. Are many schools losing a true sense of community because of the effects of corporate reform?

We already know that the breakdown of the family has created instability in children's lives. Are we going to let this happen to our schools? As mentioned in a previous chapter, if corporate "reform" is allowed to continue to dismantle public education, teachers can be fired and schools can be ruthlessly shut down because they haven't achieved unrealistic, mandated goals. This has already happened in schools across the nation. Do we want such instability in our schools? For some students, schools are the only sense of community or stability in their lives.

A friend of mine recently stated that she is dismayed by what is happening to American society. She believes that we are becoming a nation of polarized, self-serving individuals who use bullying tactics to get what we want; individuals interested only in personal gratification, without any real concern for others. Corporate reform is fueling the situation.

The likes of Bill and Melinda Gates, Eli and Edythe Broad, the Walton family, and the Koch brothers believe they have the right— and the money—to muscle their way into America's public education system and "reform" it to suit their own self-serving purposes. And, while they fill their corporate coffers, I think of my colleagues, teachers, and students around the nation, who have become corp-ses nailed into coffin-like classrooms— the life sucked out of them by corporate reform measures. It is crucial that educators speak up and be counted.

The United Opt Out National movement in California is doing just that. Comprising parents, educators, students, and activists, it has been collaborating with the Occupy Wall Street protest movement to make specific demands regarding school reform. The document being advanced by the Opt Out group states:

We believe that **QUALITY PUBLIC EDUCATION** *is a democratic right for all persons. It is through vibrant and fully funded school communities that all children have the opportunity to develop and grow into happy, successful, free, and active citizens. High stakes testing functions in opposition to* **QUALITY PUBLIC EDUCATION***, as it is used to punish children, to malign educators, and to provide financial gain for testing corporations and their sponsors.*

THEREFORE, WE DEMAND AN END TO THE FOLLOWING:

- ALL high stakes testing and punitive policies that label schools, punish students, and close public community schools.
- ALL high stakes testing that ties teacher evaluations, pay, and job security to high stakes test results.
- Corporate interventions in public education and education policy.
- The use of public education funds to enact school "choice" measures influenced and supported by the corporate agenda.
- Economically and racially segregated school communities.
- "Model" legislation that provides special rules to charter schools that are forced upon public schools.
- Corporate run for-profit charter schools that divert public funds away from public schools.
- Mandates requiring teachers to use corporate approved, scripted programs that sublimate and negate authentic and meaningful learning experiences imparted by varied and rich curricula.[81] (p. 2-5).

It is vital for more groups like United Opt Out National to organize and voice their concerns so that corporations and policy makers are not allowed to reform the system to suit their own agendas. The stark reality is that the American school system has been hijacked by the corporate world, and teachers and students are its collateral damage. Do we want corporate executives to lead the conversation about where public education is headed? I say "no."

Chapter Eight
No Conversation Left Behind
"Chalk Talk"

While my friend Doug (the high school English teacher who inspired me to become a teacher) and I were waiting for our food at a tapas restaurant, he gave me an article to read about a new private school. The article stated that students aren't allowed to bring cellphones, smartphones, laptops, iPods, iPads, or other technological devices to school. They must arrive armed only with their brains, imagination, and ingenuity. The curriculum is based on fundamentals, such as critical thinking, reading, writing, and arithmetic, but includes practical life-skills designed to produce outstanding citizens rather than outstanding test-takers. Recess is mandatory twice a day to allow students to achieve both mind-body balance and to allow students to learn life's lessons from each other. Lessons to be learned include how to communicate face-to-face, how to win and lose graciously, and how to foster teamwork and settle differences. Students also take mandatory physical education classes, foreign languages, art, dancing, music, drama, yoga and meditation, spiritual philosophies, nutrition and fitness, and woodwork and metals. All students read books, write papers, and take non-standardized tests to measure progress.[1]

I became animated and asked Doug where this school was located because I wanted to apply for a teaching job there. He told me to calm down and finish reading the article. There was a "catch." Scott Smith ended his description of this paradisiacal school by stating that The Practical Academy, for the moment, was located only in his imagination.[2]

I snapped back to reality. Promise hung in the air, because if ordinary citizen Scott Smith could be voicing such insightful ideas about what education could and should be, maybe other individuals had opinions that they'd like to voice. So, let the conversation begin!

As this statement tripped off my tongue, I felt deflated. My experiences and observations of American society over the past thirteen years told me that many Americans are losing the ability to have conversations with each other. The art of conversation has sorely diminished. These days, you'll be hard-pressed to find someone willing to listen objectively to another person's point of view and allow them to have a different opinion without taking personal offense. How many people will think critically about an issue before developing an opinion, or remain open-minded and objective while having a conversation? In today's society, many people are uninterested in the art of listening to different opinions to learn, and they are unwilling to question personal belief systems or accept compromise.

I recall several recent examples of "dysfunctional conversations." Although I opened a Facebook account four years ago, I rarely use it because I think that it's addictive and that it fuels self-absorption. However, since I haven't closed the account, people's comments filter through to my email address, and I became curious about one "conversation" between individuals across the country. Several people were upset about the Supreme Court's upholding of Obamacare, so they posted Hitler-like pictures of Obama with the word "Fascist" as caption. Another person then suggested that the individuals who posted the pictures were too young to understand how "un-American" their posts were. The response was to call this person a derogatory term! Other individuals pushed the "Like" button under this comment. I couldn't believe the faceless Facebook venom they were hurling at each other in cyberspace—and these people were relatives!

I experienced another such interaction while channel surfing on TV. I happened upon the Bill O'Reilly show and was curious about the shouting match between O'Reilly and several guests. I didn't know who the guests were but soon realized it didn't matter because I couldn't hear a word anyone said. The dysfunctional interaction intrigued me. The two guests kept trying to get their viewpoints across while O'Reilly shouted over them. Finally, O'Reilly shouted something to the effect that teachers and the public education system were responsible for the growing numbers of entitled, irresponsible citizens within the U.S. He then added his usual, "Well, gotta run now," and the show ended.[3] I sat in my chair dazed.

Although I agreed with O'Reilly about our entitlement society, I also knew that the issue was more complicated than to single-mindedly blame teachers and the education system. There are other cultural factors involved, but none of these were addressed. What disturbed me was that he wouldn't allow his guests to participate in a conversation on the topic. We viewers were exposed to a self-righteous, simplistic one-sided rant rather than a conversation.

Sadly, the media, social networking, and the American political arena are role models and re-enforcers of such an approach to human interaction. Infamous radio/TV commentators create a "them vs. us" mentality, and partisan media is now the rule rather than the exception. The partisan Congress fortifies this nationwide inability to have true conversations. Also, when teachers and schools are curbed from discussing controversial issues with students, an opportunity is lost to teach students how to have meaningful conversations about important issues.

The public education system should be a vehicle for enabling children to become responsible, clear thinking, independent adults with a balanced approach to life, so it is critical to have a conversation about changing the system. For my part of the conversation, I can contribute recommendations from the perspective of a teacher who has remained in the classroom for thirty-eight years, has taught a variety of different subjects from fifth to twelfth grade, and has taught in two countries in various school environments. From this vantage point, and from the extensive research that I have conducted, I believe that teachers should be joined in this conversation by learned experts in child psychology, learning theory, human behavior, pedagogy, knowledge transfer, and the art of teaching, learning, and curriculum development. Politicians, government officials, and corporate leaders, with their hidden agendas and vested interests, should not be included. They are the ones who need to learn to listen.

Change is difficult, especially when it entails changing a complex, nationwide, government-administered school system that has already gone through a number of failed reforms. Change usually meets resistance, especially from those with vested interests. Resistance will certainly come from politicians, government officials, and corporate leaders who have contributed to making the education system what it is today, as well as from parents and students who have acclimatized to a system that allows them to demand "rights" and make decisions that aren't necessarily sound education-wise. The wellbeing of the nation depends upon our forging ahead. To do so, I offer the following recommendations:

ACKNOWLEDGE THAT THE SYSTEM ISN'T WORKING

The first step to creating change is to acknowledge that the system isn't working despite two decades of reforms:

> The United States, like many other Anglo-American nations, has epitomized Einstein's definition of madness: keep doing the same thing while expecting to get a different result. Force, pressure, shame, top-down intervention, markets, competition, standardization, testing, and easier and quicker passages into teaching, closure of failing schools, the firing of ineffective teachers and principals, and fresh starts with young teachers and newly established schools—the very reform strategies that have failed dismally over two decades in many Anglo-Saxon nations—are being reinvented and re-imposed with even greater force and determination.[4] (p. xv).

It seemed that in 2005 a light was beginning to appear at the end of the tunnel. After almost a decade of product-oriented education and of frustrated educators trying to comply with NCLB regulations, "stakeholders" such as The Partnership for 21st Century Skills realized that the NCLB reform wasn't working.

The Partnership for 21st Century Skills was a network of nearly thirty major businesses and education groups. They came up with "21st Century Learning" as the latest paradigm, the latest buzz phrase, to reframe American education. The U.S. Conference of Mayors in 2005 passed a policy resolution supporting a framework of more comprehensive twenty-first century skills than provided by NCLB.[5]

A familiar pattern in the history of education was recurring. The pendulum of education was swinging from an emphasis on product (knowledge of facts, information, and content) to an emphasis on process (analysis, critical thinking, and cooperative learning). The consensus among many leaders in business, government, and higher education was that the intellectual and technological demands of the twenty-first century global economy required students to be able to do more than meet proficiency goals on state standardized tests. They believed that college students, workers, and citizens must be able to solve complex problems by exercising higher-level thinking skills, by thinking creatively, by generating original ideas, and by collaborating and communicating effectively.[6]

In theory, the skill focus was shifting from how much knowledge students acquire to what students do with that acquired knowledge. These skills aren't new but have taken on a new urgency in the twenty-first century, according to Elena Silva, senior policy analyst at Education Sector, an independent, nonprofit, nonpartisan think tank that challenges conventional thinking in education policy.[7]

According to The Partnership for 21st Century Skills (the main advocacy group for twenty-first century learning skills), "every 21st Century Skills implementation will require development of core academic subject knowledge and understanding among all students."[8] The Partnership developed a Framework for 21st Century Learning that describes the skills, knowledge, expertise, and literacies students must master to succeed in work and life. The Partnership's rationale was that "when a school or district builds on this foundation, combining the entire Framework with the necessary support systems—standards, assessments, curriculum and instruction, professional development and learning environments—students are more engaged in the learning process and graduate better prepared to thrive in today's global economy."[9]

Once again, teachers in districts that embraced "21st Century Learning" had to adapt their teaching strategies to suit the fashion of the moment. Many professional development courses within these districts were devoted to training teachers about the variety of technological programs and tools that they could (and were often required) to use in the classroom because digital literacy was a pillar of the paradigm.

At a glance, the paradigm is trendy and impressive with its focus on technology. Its definition of education as a process instead of a product—and its focus on higher-level thinking skills—is probably a welcome relief to educators frustrated with NCLB. The problem with the model is that it is couched in the NCLB reform, the "Race to the Top" policy, and a corporate framework, making the transition complicated. States are still required to implement standardized tests each year, and schools must still reach AYP benchmarks. Teachers must also show student growth data each year to prove their effectiveness as educators. In many states, such growth is part of teacher evaluation and merit pay systems. Parents and students are still the customers that teachers and schools must satisfy in the marketplace of education.

In earlier chapters, I discussed how our narcissistic, entitlement culture is crippling education. In addition, I pointed out how social technology and over-involvement with technology are affecting students' cognitive development. Censorship has constrained students' higher-level thinking skills, and the corporate mentality has undermined educators in the classroom. Also, twenty-first century education is oriented towards preparing students for jobs so that the U.S. can compete in the global economy, which reeks of education for the sake of hidden agendas rather than education for the sake of students.

A new vision for public education is clearly needed. A systemic change is crucial, keeping in mind that a government can't *force* its citizenry to become educated. Education should embrace and empower the human spirit, not scrutinize and punish it. The system should cultivate trust, enhance autonomy, and tolerate diversity, while creating a relaxed and fear-free learning environment built on teachers' professionalism and students' strengths.

DEVELOP A NEW PHILOSOPHICAL FRAMEWORK

A framework that understands the stages of human development and learning is needed to replace the corporate framework. Psychologist Erik Erikson's "Stages of Human Development" is a well-respected theory that explains the psychosocial process for individuals over a lifespan, highlighting the impact of social experience on personality development.[10]

Even though Erikson's stages focus on personality development throughout a lifespan, they address the importance of developing trust, independence, motivation, industry, and autonomy that are often "sound-bites" or platitudes in today's world of education.[11]

A hurdle to overcome is the replacement of debilitating strategies such as coddling, monitoring, rescuing, and indulging students to make sure they succeed. Helicopter parenting and teaching must give way to students being allowed the freedom to make mistakes, to fail, to take responsibility for their actions, and to stand by their choices and commitments. Such a change will set children on a psychologically healthy path to becoming young adults who can take responsibility for their lives. To achieve this, parents and educators must establish a balance between setting boundaries and guiding children and allowing them to increasingly assert themselves and make decisions which suit their levels of cognition. Erikson's model is a useful guideline for establishing such a balance; trust in the professionalism of teachers is key.

LEARN FROM OTHER COUNTRIES

Finland is an example of a country with a highly successful world-class education system whose philosophical approach is opposite of the American system. The Finnish system foregoes school inspection, a standardized curriculum, high-stakes student assessments, test-based accountability, and a "race-to-the-top" mentality. Teachers control the curriculum, student assessment, and school improvement. They are also free to exercise their professional knowledge and judgment in their schools.[12] Finland education focuses on:

- Being inclusive and creative.
- Developing a broad national curriculum which allows schools to adapt standards to suit school cultures.
- Developing high-quality, well-trained teachers with good academic qualifications.
- Drawing teachers into teaching because of the profession's societal mission.
- Valuing teachers' professionalism by giving them

autonomy, yet support.

- Trusting teachers' professional opinions and decisions.
- Creating professional development programs for teachers that have shifted from centralized in-service programs to programs that meet the authentic demands and expectations of schools and individuals.
- Encouraging teachers to explore their own conceptions of learning, to develop teaching methods to match their own learning theories, and to craft pedagogical environments to meet their students' needs.
- Allowing teachers to collectively develop curriculum and diagnostic assessment rather than expecting them to deliver prescribed, packaged curricula.
- Dismissing ideas of accountability and merit pay because teachers' professionalism is trusted.
- Maintaining schools as "centers of learning and caring" rather than worrying about frequent testing, competition with other schools, performance standards imposed by administrators and policy makers, and their world ranking.
- Supporting all students some time with special education strategies rather than legally identifying and labeling special education students.
- Establishing a shorter school day and school year than that within the American system.
- Linking education to creative development of economic competitiveness along with social cohesion and inclusiveness.
- Remaining immune to market-based education reform.
- Disallowing standardized tests except for the National Metriculation Exam, which everyone takes at the end of a voluntary upper-secondary school.
- Giving all students report cards at the end of each semester based on individualized grading.

- Periodically tracking national progress by testing a few sample groups across a range of different schools.
- Distributing resources equitably among schools rather than basing distribution on competition and choice.
- Discouraging private schools with tuition because Finland wants to give every child the opportunity for an equitable education.
- Dismissing school choice and engagement with the private sector as a viable education option.
- Encouraging cooperation rather than competition between schools and between teachers.[13]

Finland uses a "means justifies the ends" approach that carefully selects "means" that don't necessarily lead to predetermined outcomes. This approach is similar to that of open-minded parents who have no preconceived ideas about who and/or what their children become, guiding them as they grow into adulthood, understanding that genetic and environmental factors also influence the outcome. By contrast, the U.S. approach is an "ends justifies the means" one that incorporates whatever means needed to achieve predetermined outcomes—whether or not these are sound. Such an approach is similar to that of close-minded parents who have preconceived ideas about who and/or what they want their children to become, monitoring them as they grow into adulthood.

The Finnish system is also exemplary because the focus is truly on the individual child's educational journey. Education is viewed as an intrinsic process and a "state of being" rather than a product to be acquired. To implement elements of the Finnish paradigm, the U.S. would need to end its unhealthy obsession with being number one in everything, its fear of uncertainty, its "one size fits all" approach to education, its belief that statistics measure learning, its focus on competition and pitting schools and teachers against each other, its blame of teachers for a dysfunctional education system, and its policy of controlling student outcomes nationwide. Such changes, however, would require a psychological shift in the American psyche.

As for the American love of competition, the Finnish writer Samuli Paronen says, "Real winners do not compete."[14] This unthinkable Finnish attitude might have merit if the U.S. is serious about no child being left behind.

Critics of the Finnish system claim that transforming the American system along Finnish lines is not feasible because Finland is a small, homogenous country compared to the U.S. This is true. However, if the American system was decentralized and each state was given control over its own educational destiny, the Finnish approach could work because states could develop policies to suit social, cultural, and economic geographies.

PURPOSE OF AMERICAN EDUCATION

American public education should do more than prepare students for the workforce or global economy. It should be available to all Americans and prepare them for life by giving them the knowledge and skills needed to responsibly participate in a democratic society, to solve personal problems, and to make informed decisions about issues confronting them. Ideally, public education should strive to make students lifelong, independent learners.

TRANSFORMATION FROM CORPORATE FRAMEWORK

We need to stop the "corporatization" of the American school system. This can be achieved if we address these key points:

- Remind ourselves that schools are not a business but a public good.
- Focus on education for its own sake rather than for ulterior motives or to indulge vested interests within a community or the nation.
- Decentralize the school system. Return management and control of education to states and local school districts and communities, focusing on schools as the center of community involvement where trust and communication can develop between educators, parents, students, and other organizations—business and otherwise.
- Maintain national and state standards in subject areas but allow districts, communities, and states the autonomy to

implement them to suit their geographical, cultural, and social environments.

- Distribute national and state funding equitably rather than award it competitively between states and districts where districts that lose the "race to the top" are penalized while those that win are rewarded.
- Abolish state/national standardized testing.
- Allow teachers to collectively develop curriculum and diagnostic assessments rather than expecting them to deliver prescribed, packaged curricula.
- Allow teachers to collaborate within their educational communities to develop a variety of student assessment tools that assess the entire spectrum of public school education: academic, physical, social, moral, digital, artistic. Multi-modal assessment should be used, including teacher prepared tests, portfolios, projects, observation, quizzes, journals, oral presentations, performance-based presentations, self-reflection, self-assessment, conferencing, visual presentations, experiments which assess both formative and summative learning.
- Abolish the market-driven idea of choicing in and out of public schools. Students should attend designated local schools and make the best of them –learning about the commitment needed to be a member of a community or work within designated schools to improve them.
- Abolish school report cards because they pit schools against each other and create an atmosphere of animosity and unhealthy competition, leading to schools having to compromise themselves and resort to desperate means to keep and/or solicit students to attend said schools. Remember the issue is to evaluate the individual student and deal with his strengths and weaknesses.
- Do not base teachers' pay on "merit" and standardized test results but on their professional standing within a community the way other professionals such as doctors, lawyers, architects, judges, psychiatrists, engineers, etc. are paid who don't have to prove their worth/legitimacy within their professions.

- Treat teachers as the professionals they are and pay them according to their years of experience as educators rather than to honor only a minimal number of years of experience on the pay scale if they choose to move to a different school district or state.
- Train principals and administrators in the field of education and require them to spend at least ten years in the classroom to qualify for such positions. They should also have to teach at least one class per day every year to keep them in touch with what is happening in the classroom.
- Back teachers when they are confronted by unreasonable students and parents if teachers are to regain their professional status, respect, and autonomy within the classroom. This does not mean that a teacher is never wrong; but it does mean that the market-driven idea that schools must please parents and students and meet their demands because they are the "clients" must change because parents and students don't usually qualify as educators or always come from a position of what is really best for students.
- Require that every school at every level has a well-conceived, coherent, sequential curriculum based on broad-based national curriculum standards whose intentions are to educate children in the liberal arts and the sciences, as well as physical education where they learn not only academic skills but the social skills needed to live within a community: commitment, responsibility, tolerance, empathy, reliability, flexibility, respect, open-mindedness, cooperation, active participation, and constructive communication.
- Accept and honor the fact that children have different abilities. Pay more than lip service to Howard's classification of multiple intelligences (bodily-kinesthetic, musical, spatial, linguistic, logical-mathematical, interpersonal, and intrapersonal) by developing a graduated/tiered curriculum that allows students to specialize as they progress within the system.
- Make the goal of evaluation and assessment to identify which students and schools need help, then go to whatever lengths necessary to help them, rather than punish them by firing

teachers, putting schools on punitive improvement plans, or shutting schools down if they don't improve.

- Allow students to fail because failure is one of life's lessons. Doing so does not mean that educators neglect students who are failing, but it does mean that they must not overcompensate for students in order to get them to pass. Students fail tasks and subjects for a variety of reasons such as procrastination, lack of interest, lack of motivation, retribution as well as lack of ability, and they can learn from their mistakes by not being rescued from such failure. They can also gain a clearer perspective of their individual weaknesses as well as strengths.

- Acknowledge that not every student is "college oriented" and that a tiered/graduated system that also offers apprentice-ships, vocational training, and any other form of education that truly honors students' individuality should be implemented to honor diversity.

- Incorporate appropriate age level use of technology in the classroom, based on current psychological and educational research about the effects of technology on children's abilities to think, concentrate, and learn at various stages of development.

- Challenge students with reading material that hasn't been censored for politically left or right wing reasons; doing so will develop deeper level thinking skills.

- Underpin education with creativity because it is a quintessential human attribute and is core to how we express ourselves. The critical role of imagination, discovery, and creativity in students' education and in their lives should not be underestimated, especially within the educational environment. Today's children must be given the chance to develop their creativity to its fullest; not only for their own benefit but also for the benefit of the communities they inhabit.

The above recommendations would transform the system from a corporate entity back to that of a community-oriented institution.

Over the past decade, Americans have experienced 911, Hurricane Katrina, the economic meltdown, the oil spill, and

Hurricane Sandy—natural and national disasters on a grand scale. None, however, is as pervasive and as insidious as the disaster in American education. An education system is the backbone of a society, and if it has become dysfunctional, it needs to be fixed.

Chapter Nine
No Creativity Left Behind
"Putting the FUN Back into DysFUNction"

The three little pigs are hungry and call the wolf to see if he wants to come for dinner. Of course, their real motive is to eat him for dinner. They'd invited him several times before, but the wolf had always managed to escape. When he arrives, the pigs once again shove the wolf into the oven, put an apple in his mouth, and head to the grocery store to get applesauce to have with their roast wolf. The wolf escapes and flees the scene, another apple in tow. Discouraged by the wolf's escape, the pigs finally give up on having roast wolf for dinner. One of them asks the others if they feel like hamburger. The scene ends with his saying into the phone, "Hey, Mr. Cow, would you like to join us for dinner." . . .

After reading the fractured fairytale "Goldilocks on Trial" and discussing the elements of fairytales and storylines, my sixth grade drama class was divided into groups and given scenarios from which to create "fractured fairytales." One group's scenario stated, "Tell the story of the 'Three Little Pigs' so that the three wolf-eating pigs go after the defenseless wolf." I was amazed at the group's sophisticated, humorous, and creative result recounted above.

Similarly, my seventh grade drama classes were given mime scenes. One group was given the topic, "At the beach." Their story was of kids surfing, picnicking, playing volleyball, and building sand castles. At the climax of the story, a shark begins surfing with a kid. The others rescue the surfer by punching the shark in the jaw, and they continue their fun in the sun. The wonderful aspect to this performance was the inventive props. The ocean consisted of chairs lined up with their backs facing the audience and a light blue piece of fabric draped over them. A cardboard shark was attached to a stick, and a student manipulated it behind the ocean of chairs while a surfer surfed on the wave of chairs. When given the chance, students' resourcefulness is unending.

Despite frustrations, I'm probably one of the luckiest teachers alive because my field is drama. Each day I marvel at students' spontaneity and enthusiasm. Each day I marvel at the clever ideas that flow from them. Each day I marvel at their ability to make connections. This euphoria, however, will inevitably be dampened when 50% of a teacher's evaluation will depend on data collection each quarter that demonstrates students have shown "growth" in drama. Gloom and doom were expressed by the creative arts' teachers in my district who met to discuss the new coporate style evaluation process. It isn't that we're opposed to assessing students because we gladly do so all the time. But, such data collection is anathema to the creative process. It shifts the focus from process to product, so teachers end up spending precious time collecting data for education and government bureaucrats. There is also the dilemma of how one quantitatively evaluates "growth" in creativity.

Paradoxically though, as I have indicated before, "creativity" is supposed to be a priority of "21st Century Learning Skills" and would be a boon to those in the arts who have always made creativity a number one priority. However, as explored in previous chapters, the current system encourages conformity and imitation rather than spontaneity and creativity. Standardized testing can kill creativity because creativity is a way of being—a process—not a product, and it must be treated as such.

According to Dr. Ashfaq Ishaq, founder of the International Child Art Foundation, traditional schooling does not generally foster children's creativity. In fact, research shows that there is a "fourth grade slump" across cultures. Dr. Ishaq states:

> Data indicates that when children begin school
> their level of creativity is evident and often flourish-
> ing. By the time they reach the fourth grade, however,
> they have become more conforming, less likely to
> take risks, and less playful or spontaneous than in
> earlier years. These trends continue throughout

the school years and into adulthood. Hence the risk of diminishing creativity faced by children needs to be addressed by adults, if humans are to attain their creative potential.[1]

Environmental influences may partially explain why childhood creativity can be a poor predictor of adult creativity and that most young children are very creative. However, creativity diminishes by 40% between the ages of five and seven when formal schooling begins, and there is some agreement that formal education inhibits the transformation of early talent into adult creativity.[2]

Creativity guru Csikszentmihalyi adds an important perspective, stating that "centers of creativity tend to be at the intersection of different cultures, where beliefs, lifestyles, and knowledge mingle and allow individuals to see new combinations of ideas with greater ease."[3] However, he observes, it's harder to achieve creativity and new ways of thinking within uniform and rigid cultures. Because the culture within American schools is uniform and rigid, and because we live in an age for bookkeepers rather than innovators, Csikszentmihalyi claims that if we want the next generation to face the future with self-confidence and the ability to think critically and creatively, we must educate them to be original as well as competent. Only time will tell whether creativity is truly a priority within American education.[4]

After twenty-five years of teaching drama at all levels of secondary school, I'm more than convinced that creativity is a driving, fundamental force. Throughout history, individuals and groups have acted on their own creative impulses to produce ideas, inventions, works of art, and entire cultures. I always discuss with my drama students how it is human nature to create and to play. There is evidence of this as far back as tribal times when humans told stories, created myths, and performed rituals and ceremonies about events in their lives. When children "play" they unconsciously act out experiences in their lives which are often based on their observations of the adult world. Adults continue to act out human experiences via theater productions, films, musicals, and dance which are in essence forms of play. Other activities such as vacations, sports, and hobbies affirm the importance of play and creativity in our lives.

Medical doctor and psychiatrist Stuart Brown claims that humans are biologically programed to "play" throughout their entire life cycle. Forty years of research and field work led him to the conclusion that "play" helps the brain adapt and improvise when unexpected challenges arise. Brown conducted "play histories" of six thousand people, including Nobel Laureates to hardened criminals. He found that some of the richest histories of play were those individuals who were high achievers in business, science, and the arts. Brown concluded that "many successful people have maintained a common thread between early natural play tendencies and what they do in their adult lives."[5]

The key to transforming public education lies with initiating creativity programs in schools for students, educators, and parents. Sir Ken Robinson, noted for his work in the field of creativity, speaking at a TED conference about creativity, stated that education systems around the world are "educating people out of their creative capacities" because as individuals progress through schools "only their heads" become the focus, and individuals inevitably "grow out of creativity." Sir Ken emphasized the importance of changing this state of affairs by focusing on the richness of human capacity which unveils itself through creative expression.[6]

Being creative is more basic to our existence than are the traditional 3 R's—reading, writing, and 'rithmetic which are public education's focus. It's critical that we create learning environments that inspire individuals to grow creatively because doing so is a step towards transforming the current product-driven system. Within such environments, educators must be allowed to express their own personal and professional creativity because they are models for their students. If they are not in touch with the creative process, it's unlikely that they will effectively ignite creativity in their students.

Students are introduced to the learning process and to the socializing process, but seldom to the creative process. Teachers develop "creative" lessons ad hoc and not because creativity has been deemed an essential life skill to be developed. "Creativity for its own sake" needs to become an important part of a school's curriculum—equivalent to reading, writing, math, and computer literacy skills. Schools need to set aside time during the day or week to focus on activities to get students' creativity flowing, not as an extension of academic work, or to evaluate students' creativity, or to collect data to demonstrate their growth. Schools designate time for reinforcement of reading, writing, and arithmetic skills, so why not for creativity? Such activities should exclude the use of technology so that students get in touch with their innately creative spirits.

It would be advantageous for districts to hire creativity specialists, similar to the hiring of literacy, special needs, and talented and gifted specialists, whose function would be to develop creativity programs within schools at all levels, to help facilitate such programs, and to act as collaborators to teachers who are implementing these programs. Districts also need to offer creativity professional development classes for educators. Educators have had to deliver packaged curricula and to take prescribed professional development classes for so long that offering such classes would allow them to break out of their straitjackets. Teacher training programs need to follow suit.

In April of 2005, I offered a professional development course in creativity for educators. We did a variety of activities to ignite or re-ignite personal creativity. We danced, we sang, we painted, we drummed, we played assimilation games, we wrote, we reflected, we embraced the creative process, exploring the depths of what it means to "create." An amazing dynamics developed among participants. We bonded from our opportunity to share spontaneously and enthusiastically, to be personally creative, and to laugh heartily. At the end of each session, participants shared creative activities they did outside of the classroom, whether it was card- making, singing, dancing, photography, art, writing, or cake-decorating.

At the beginning of the next school year, many of the teachers who had taken the course begged me to offer it again, claiming that it was one of the best professional development courses they had taken. They loved the relaxed, open atmosphere and camaraderie that had developed among us. Some of them said that they felt deflated when the course finished. It had been therapeutic because it relieved stress and, in a positive way, momentarily freed them from their everyday concerns. By igniting their own personal creativity they felt more confident to stimulate creativity in their students. Some of them had come into the class claiming they weren't creative, but left realizing that we all are. I realized after teaching the course just how often teachers' individual needs are neglected.

After experiencing teachers' aliveness when allowed to "be creative," I wanted to make a difference in their lives. I decided to get my master's degree in adult education and develop a creativity course for educators. If doing so could empower and reinvigorate teachers, then my career shift would be meaningful. I remembered talking to a number of teachers at conferences I had attended around the country and how disillusioned many of them felt about their profession.

One woman in Virginia Beach had been a substitute teacher and thought about becoming a teacher but decided not to because the teachers at the schools where she worked were subdued. A forty--something woman in Denver had just finished student teaching and decided not to continue, seeing that her focus would not be on curriculum (her passion), kids, and the classroom because policy-driven, bureaucratic red tape restricted her. A young teacher at a creativity conference in New York said she doubted she would teach more than a few years. She felt like a prostitute because of the way parents and students were allowed to treat her and her colleagues. A teacher at a creativity conference in Santa Fe decided to quit in the middle of a school year. After thirty years of teaching, she couldn't stand it any longer. She felt burdened and stressed by the bureaucratic tasks, data collection, and record-keeping that impinged on her teaching. She quit and created a blog in support of teachers.

Not all teachers feel disenfranchised or stressed. Some may be unaware of their stress until health-related issues surface. Such was the case with one teacher whose doctor attributed her onset of multiple sclerosis to stress in the workplace. Still others may take a pragmatic approach to teaching and accept the education system as is. However, there is enough disillusionment to warrant exploring ways to develop higher job satisfaction. Offering creativity courses would allow teachers to experience a sense of play, dampen the daily stress, and allow them to enhance their own creativity which could be modeled for students.

In recent years, researchers, managers, and employers have realized the importance of establishing creative, inclusive work environments that value, trust, and respect employees' abilities and input. Doing so leads to more intrinsically motivated employees with higher job satisfaction, leading to employee retention as well as the generation of new ideas. Not doing so often kills creativity and new ideas and innovation.[7] A case in point is Google. Google has been on Fortune magazine's list of *100 Best Companies to Work For* every year since 2007 when it was only a seven-year-old internet communications and technology company. The company is noted for its creative work environment and its focus on workplace flexibility, productivity, and creativity. The company's goal is to create the happiest, most productive workplace in the world, and it believes that it will achieve this goal by truly looking after its workers by giving them the time and space to be creative.

Queen's University in Canada decided to modify the workplace through regular art-making sessions with staff members. Over time, the university community explored a variety of paint and mixed-media as well as collage. Participants gained a sense of community and both professional and personal benefits. Some individuals claimed to have gained energy, enthusiasm, and boldness and were able to apply these to their academic work. The rationale for this project was that even though educators nurture others, caring for educators is often neglected.[8]

Other educational institutions have followed Queens University. Morely College, a center for adult education, is known for nurturing creativity in adults and has become a strong forum for the articulation of individuals' desires and aspirations outside the work environment. The college seeks to "fill gaps in education" for working men and women. Similar programs of adult education have a role to play alongside further education colleges because they provide added value, offering a step back into education for many adults.[9]

Finland acknowledges that to develop creativity schools need to have relaxed, open environments conducive to the creative process. Finnish educators understand the importance of encouraging opinions and ideas, of not relying on order and tradition, and of not making people afraid to fail. That is why competition and standardized testing are not important. Finnish schools assign less homework, have shorter school days and school years, and focus on engaging children in play. The goal is to teach students "how to learn, not how to take a test," and this goal is founded on the belief "if you only measure the statistics you miss the human aspect."[10]

Finnish teachers realize that exploration and discovery are important components of "learning how to learn," and that students need the time and space to do so. Ironically, by viewing education as a process, by allowing students and teachers to engage in that process, and by not focusing on being number one in the world, Finland is number one in education. Incredibly, even knowing this, most Finns don't care because it is not a priority. Their focus is on leading more enriched and rewarding lives and on making productive and meaningful contributions to the workplace, community, and society.

The word "creativity" evokes thoughts of a spontaneous, un-teachable process emanating from inspiration—the "ah-ha moment." During the 1970s, one trendy education philosophy allowed kids do whatever inspired them during the school day. Such an approach was opposite to today's paradigm, and it didn't last long. Since the 1970s, extensive research has been conducted on the creative process, and there are a number of strategies that teachers can use to ignite creativity in students. While teaching drama during the past twenty-five years, I have discovered a number of such strategies:

- Creating a safe environment for risk-taking, free from anxiety and time-pressure.
- Creating a personalized environment.
- Focusing on process, not product.
- Bringing the real world into classroom activities.
- Promoting self-direction and autonomy in learning.
- Appreciating children's expertise.
- Setting aside time for generating ideas.
- Encouraging a spirit of play and experimentation.
- Allowing students to make mistakes and learn from them.
- Providing a variety of stimuli and resources.
- Allowing free choice in task assignments.
- Fostering intense concentration and task commitment through high motivation and interest in self-selected topics.
- Making it possible for children to experience social creativity during group interactions and through joint projects with self-selected partners.
- Allowing for self-assessment and group-assessment.
- Providing opportunities for group interaction and sharing.

- Offering positive and constructive feedback and reality checks.
- Nurturing sensibility, flexibility, and divergent thinking.
- Encouraging and accepting constructive non-conformist behavior and original ideas.
- Exploring the use of the different senses in relation to perception.
- Developing students' intuition and perceptions via classroom activities.
- Exploring blocks to creative and critical thinking such as assumptions, generalizations, and faulty inferences that students may have about topics.
- Using Bloom's Taxonomy to guide learning activities and higher-level thinking skills.

Infusing passion and creativity into education is beneficial to students, teachers, society, and the world. Tapping into individual creativity is a springboard for individual growth and wisdom, leading to what it truly means to be "educated." In Sir Robinson's words:

> If we discover the Element in ourselves and
> encourage others to find theirs, the opportunities
> for growth are infinite. If we fail to do that, we
> may get by, but our lives will be duller as a
> result.[11] (p. 259).

Creativity's transformative nature can also heal the dysfunction within American society mirrored in our schools. All of us are born with degrees of fear and uncertainty. When we live in psychologically repressive environments, growth is curbed, and we often project these feelings onto the world rather than deal with them. This is the current state of our society and education—which isn't to say that there aren't psychologically healthy individuals in the U.S.—but there is a need to "balance the scales." The creative process can bring equilibrium.

Julia Cameron, author of *The Artist's Way* series, demonstrates a clear understanding of how the creative process can bring equilibrium. Her contributions to the field of creativity have been substantial in this regard. She understands the importance of unblocking the creative energy within individuals.[12] Students and teachers could benefit from the introduction of Cameron's process into our schools to help release blocked creativity.

Creativity requires that an individual take an exclusive journey to the recesses of the soul. This journey embraces the developmental stages of Erik Erickson's "Stages of Human Development" which includes facing fears, taking risks, making mistakes, sometimes failing, taking responsibility, being committed, and accepting that success is what life is all about.[13] This intuitive journey is a "reality check" leading towards wholeness— autonomy, balance, and wisdom. We can begin within our schools to swing the pendulum towards a healthy American psyche by nurturing individuals who can truly manifest their own destinies.

Conclusion
Leaving My Classroom Behind
"A Teary Tale"

As I have embraced the creative process while penning these pages—researching, thinking and rethinking, writing and rewriting—I realize that with completion of this book I am also completing a chapter of my life and that my retirement is eminent. I have mixed feelings about taking that final step. Such a realization reminds me of a statement made by Lillian Hellman in the film "Julia" as she reflects on her lifelong friendship with a woman of that name:

> Old paint on canvas as it ages sometimes becomes
> transparent. When that happens, in some pictures
> it is possible to see the original lines: a tree will show
> through a woman's dress; a child makes way for a
> dog; a boat is no longer on an open sea. That is
> called 'pentimento' because the painter repented,
> changed his mind. . .I want to remember what was
> there for me once and what is there for me now. . .[1]

It's hard to believe that thirty-eight years have passed. Wasn't it only yesterday that I walked into my first classroom? I never could have imagined that the day would arrive when I would no longer be a teacher. I'm proud to have dedicated these years to the profession. For most of this time, I've been in my element, believing that my contributions to education and to children had merit.

I vividly remember my first teaching job and a seventh grade girl named Melanie. She had frizzy brown hair, an olive complexion, and a beautiful smile. At the end of the year, she gave me a picture of a little girl holding a heart drawn in pink ink on green stenographer's paper. I have kept that drawing all of these years, along with other notes and gifts that students have given me. I also remember another little boy whose name escapes me. He loved to read and he wrote well, but he hated doing grammar. We always talked about the latest book he was reading, and I promised him I would read *The Phantom Tollbooth*. The next year, after I had moved to Australia, he wrote me a letter to see if I had read the book yet. To this day, I wonder about both of these students—where they are and what they are doing.

I've felt lucky that for so many years I could embrace the learning process because I've always loved to learn, and I've always had a passion for literature, drama, and the arts. I've felt honored to be able to explore great Literature with students to hopefully ignite a passion within them, too. I've loved the creative process involved in developing new lessons and new courses.

I've been lucky to teach in a variety of educational environments in both public and private schools. I've taught in the inner city, the suburbs, and out in the country. In each of these environments, I worked with dedicated teachers, many of whom are still friends today. None of us fit the scripted "effective" teacher. We all brought our own uniqueness and contributions to the learning process. The one thing we had in common was that we cared about kids and were dedicated to them. And, as I reflect, I can't say that there were more than seven or eight teachers throughout the thirty-eight years who should possibly never have become teachers.

More importantly, I remember so many students who impacted my life. I hope, in return, that I was able to impact theirs. I remember lively class discussions in language arts and literature classes where students learned not only to express their opinions but to listen to those of others. I remember taking college prep students on weekend study camps at a school camp site out in the country. I remember the phenomenal acting talent of students in school productions, the phenomenal writing talent of students in language arts' classes, and the phenomenal creativity of students in drama classes. I remember supervising students on weeklong skiing and canoeing camps. I remember taking students on numerous theater and film excursions that embellished what we were learning in class. I loved the spontaneity and aliveness of the relationships we established.

Being a teacher is in my blood. I never wanted to be a principal or an administrator. I wanted to be a teacher in the classroom with students, as have so many of my past and current colleagues. I have learned that teaching is a highly personal, dynamic experience. It's not a craft that one learns once and for all and then practices for a lifetime. It's not a skill that can be condensed into sound-bite bullet-point skills that lead to "effective" instruction. It's a complex, lifelong journey filled with unpredictable challenges, unique relationships with students, and fresh insights about subject matter and methodology. More importantly, it's about staying alive and engaged and forever remaining a student among students.

I gained the most profound insight about being a teacher when I moved to Australia and became a novice in another culture and education system. I had to navigate my way within a foreign country. Any assumptions I previously had about life were turned upside down. This experience has underpinned my teaching career. The memory of what it feels like to be a novice has guided me in the classroom when working with students who are also novices.

I wish that I could convince myself to teach for two more years so that I could have dedicated forty years to the classroom. But, as the opening sentence of L.P. Hartley's novel *The Go-Between* states, "The past is a foreign country. They do things differently there."[2] I am now a "stranger in a strange land," working within a system that has lost its way.

When I left behind my country thirty-eight years ago to teach in Australia, I anticipated feeling like a "stranger in a strange land." However, I never imagined that I would feel the same way about my career upon returning to the U.S. Sadly, I must also leave behind my classroom. I'm left wondering what current teachers will be saying about their teaching careers when they decide to leave them behind. Will we have a nation of teachers who are prepared to dedicate their lives to the profession or will teaching continue on its current path to be a temporary job that many teachers choose to leave behind before it even becomes a career?

By writing this book, I hope to reach teachers who feel similarly to me about American education so that they realize they are not alone. I also hope to articulate to government officials and policy-makers what it's really like for teachers working in the trenches of education. They and the public must be made aware of the significant issues that underlie the current problems within the system rather than blaming or holding teachers solely accountable for lack of student performance. As a teacher, I want my voice to be heard as the American education system moves forward to an uncertain future.

Let's not leave our American teachers behind and buried beneath a quagmire of ineffective, unrealistic government policies. Let's allow teachers to offer their experience and insight into the creation of an effective and enduring public education system.

Call to Action
Taking Back Our Classrooms

- Write letters to local, state, and federal legislators and politicians.
- Write letters to the President and the federal Education Secretary.
- Write letters to individuals within your school district: principals, administrators, superintendent, school board members.
- Write letters to officials and policy-makers within your state education department.
- Create local support/activist groups within your district or among teachers from districts within your town/city/rural area.
- Talk to your school's PTA members about your concerns.
- Organize other teachers within your school/district and refuse to administer tests at your school.
- Create a blog, you tube video, alone or with other concerned colleagues, expressing your concerns.
- Write articles for newspapers or education magazines.
    1. Education Week
    2. Yes! Magazine
    3. American Educator
    4. Education Next
    5. Rethinking Schools
    6. The Journal
- Join local, state, national activist groups/marches:
    1. United Opt Out: www.unitedoptout.org
    2. Education for Liberation Network: www.edliberation.org
    3. www.saveourschoolsmarch.org
    4. www.teacheractivists@gmail.com
    5. www.teacheractivistgroups.org
- Attend conferences as a speaker or participant:
    1. Free Minds, Free People Conference (www.fmfp.org).
    2. Teach to Lead summits
    3. NYCORE conferences

Notes

Chapter One
No Challenge Left Behind
"The Lay of the Land"

1. Erica Goldson, "Here I Stand: Valedictorian Speaks Out Against Schooling in Graduation Speech. www.sott.net. (accessed June 25, 2010).
2. B. Starnes, "NCLB Heads Down Alice's Rabbit Hole," *Educational Digest* 70, no. 8 (2005): 3.

Chapter Two
No Country Left Behind
"A Fear-y Tale"

1. Herman Melville, *Moby Dick* (New York: Oxford University Press, 1998).
2. Jack London, *The Call of the Wild, White Fang, and to Build a Fire* (New York: Modern Library Classics, 2012).
3. Ernest Becker, *The Denial of Death* (New York: Free Press Paperbacks, 1973).
4. Ibid, xiii.
5. Joseph Campbell, *The Power of Myth* (New York: Anchor Books, 1998).
6. Declaration of Independence
7. O.E. Rolvaag, *Giants in the Earth* (New York: Harper Perennial Publishers, 1991).
8. James Truslow Adams, *The Epic of America* (Piscataway: Transaction Publishers, 2012).
9. Philip K. Howard, *The Death of Common Sense: How Law is Suffocating America* (New York: Random House, Inc., 1994), 5.
10. "Minority Report," DVD, directed by Steven Spielberg (20th Century Fox, 2002).
11. Howard, *The Death of Common Sense*.
12. Ron Cobb, *The Cobb Book: Cartoons* (Sydney, Australia: Wild and Woolley Press, 1975).
13. Robert Pape, "Empire Falls," *The National Interest* 9 (2009): 21.
14. James Bell, "China Seen Overtaking U.S. as Global Superpower," *PEW Global Attitudes Project* (2011).
15. M. Rich, "American 15-year-olds Lag, Mainly in Math, on International Standardized Tests," *The New York Times* (2013).

16. Rich, "American 15-year-olds Lag, Mainly in Math, on International Standardized Tests."

17. "The Finland Phenomenon: Inside the World's Most Surprising School System," DVD, directed by Sean Faust (True South Studios, 2011).

Chapter Three
No Citizen Left Behind
"Contemplating Our Navels"

1. Ray Bradbury, *The Illustrated Man* (New York: Simon and Schuster; Reprint edition, 2012).

2. Ibid.

3. Imogen Tyler, "The Me Decade' to the Me Millenium': The Cultural History of Narcissism," *International Journal of Cultural Studies* 10 (2007): 343.

4. Otto Kernberg, *Borderline Conditions and Pathological Narcissism* (Lanham: Rowman and Littlefield Publishers, Inc., 1986).

5. H. Hendrick, "Optimism and Hope Versus Anxiety and Narcissism: Some Thoughts on Children's Welfare Yesterday and Today," *History of Education* 37, no. 6 (2007):747-768.

6. I. Thomson, "The Theory That Won't Die: From Mass Society to the Decline of Social Capital," *Sociological Forum* 20, no. 3 (2005): 421-448.

7. Eric Fromm, *To Have or To Be* (New York: Continuum, 1976).

8. Tyler, "The Me Decade' to the Me Millennium': The Cultural History of Narcissism," 343.

9. Christopher Lasch, *The Culture of Narcissism: American Life in a Time of Diminishing Expectations* (New York: W.W. Norton & Company, Inc., 1991).

10. J. Batton, "The 'New Narcissism' in 20th Century America: The Shadow and Substance of Social Change," *Journal of Social History* 17, no. 2 (1983): 199-220.

11. J. Twenge and W. Campbell, *The Narcissism Epidemic* (New York: Free Press, 2009).

12. Fromm, *To Have or To Be.*

13. Ibid, 5.

14. Ibid, 5.

15. Charles Dickens, *A Tale of Two Cities* (New York: Bantam Classics, 1989), 1.

16. Twenge and Campbell, *The Narcissism Epidemic.*

17. Hendrick, "Optimism and Hope Versus Anxiety and Narcissism: Some Thoughts on Children's Welfare Yesterday and Today," 747-768.

18. Tyler, "The Me Decade' to the Me Millennium': The Cultural History of Narcissism," 343.
19. Hendrick, "Optimism and Hope Versus Anxiety and Narcissism: Some Thoughts on Children's Welfare Yesterday and Today," 747-768.
20. Twenge and Campbell, *The Narcissism Epidemic.*
21. Hendrick, "Optimism and Hope Versus Anxiety and Narcissism: Some Thoughts on Children's Welfare Yesterday and Today," 747-768.
22. Tyler, "The Me Decade' to the Me Millennium': The Cultural History of Narcissism," 343.
23. Twenge and Campbell, *The Narcissism Epidemic.*
24. Tyler, "The Me Decade' to the Me Millennium': The Cultural History of Narcissism," 343.
25. Hara Estroff Marano, *A Nation of Whimps* (New York: Broadway Books 2008).
26. Twenge and Campbell, *The Narcissism Epidemic.*
27. Polly Young-Eisendreth, *The Self-esteem Trap* (Boston: Little Brown and Company, 2005).
28. Twenge and Campbell, *The Narcissism Epidemic.*
29. Marano, *A Nation of Whimps.*
30. E. Greenberger, J. Lessard, C. Chen, S. Farrugia, "Self-entitled College Students: Contributions of Personality, Parenting, and Motivational Factors," *Journal of Youth Adolescence* 37, (2008): 1193-1204.
31. E. Correa, "Pedagogy of the Obsessed: Shifting the Focus," *College Quarterly* 9, no. 3 (2006): 1-2.
32. L. Lum, "Handling Helicopter Parents," *Diverse: Issues in Higher Education* 23, no. 20 (2006): 40-43.
33. E. Wills, "Parent Trap," *The Chronicle of Higher Education* 5, no. 46 (2005): 1-2.
34. Marano, *A Nation of Whimps.*
35. Lum, "Handling Helicopter Parents," 40-43.
36. Wills, "Parent Trap," 1-2.
37. Marano, *A Nation of Whimps.*
38. J. Le Leau, "The 'Silver spoon' Syndrome in the Super Rich: The Pathological Linkage of Affluence and Narcissism in Family Systems," *American Journal of Psychotherapy* 52, no. 3 (1988): 425-43.
39. Young-Eisendrath, *The Self-esteem Trap.*
40. Marano, *A Nation of Whimps.*
41. J. Abbott, P. Leith, & H. MacTaggart, *Over-schooled but Undereducated: How the Crisis in Education is Jeopardizing Our*

Adolescent (New York: Continuum International Publishing Group, 2010), xxiii-xxiv.

42. Interview with psychologist, Dr. Shirley Robbins, February 4, 2010.

Chapter Four
No Cellphone Left Behind
"Techno-toiletries Run Rampant"

1. M. Leunig, *The Penguin Leunig* (Camberwell, VIC, Australia: Penguin Group, 1974).
2. Ibid.
3. "Being There," DVD, directed by Hal Ashby (Warner Bros., 1979).
4. A. Lenhart, "Teens, Cell Phones and Texting: Text Messaging Becomes Centerpiece of Communication," *Pew Internet and American Life Project* (2010).
5. Kaiser Family Foundation, "Study Shows Kids Tethered to Technology," http://abcnes.go.com/WN/kids-electronics-study-shows- kids-spend-hours-day/story?id=9...(accessed Jan. 20, 2010).
6. Mark Bauerlein, *The Dumbest Generation: How the Digital Age Stupefies Young Americans and Jeopardizes Our Future* (New York: W.W. Norton and Company, Inc., 2008).
7. Janet Healy, *Failure to Connect: How Computers Affect Our Children's Minds—and What We Can Do about It* (New York: Simon & Schuster Paperbacks, 1998).
8. P. Klorer, "The Effects of Technological Overload on Children: An Art Therapist's Perspective," *Art Therapy: Journal of the American Art Therapy Association* 26, no. 2 (2009): 80-82.
9. Henry Giroux, *Education and the Crisis of Public Values: Challenging the Assault on Teachers, Students, and Public Education* (New York: Peter Lang Publishing, Inc., 2012).
10. Robert Ornstein, *The Evolution of Consciousness: The Origin of the Way We Think* (New York: Simon & Schuster Paperbacks, 1991).
11. Nicholas Carr, *The Shallows: What the Internet is Doing to Our Brains* (New York: W.W. Norton & Company, Inc., 2010).
12. Maggie Jackson, *Distracted: The Erosion of Attention and the Coming Dark Age* (Amherst: Prometheus Books, 2008), 13.
13. Ibid.
14. Ibid.
15. William James, *The Principles of Psychology* (Mineola: Dover Publications, 1950), 404.

16. Mihaly Csikszentmihalyc, *Finding Flow: The Psychology of Engagement with Everyday Life* (New York: Basic Books, 1997).
17. A. Pascuel-Leone, A. Amedi, F. Fregni, & B. Merabet, "The Plastic Human Brain Cortex," *Annual Review of Neuroscience* 28 (2005): 377-401.
18. Carr, *The Shallows*.
19. Healy, *Failure to Connect*.
20. Jackson, *Distracted*, 18.
21. Carr, *The Shallows*, 57.
22. N. Baron, *Always on: Language in an Online and Mobile World* (Oxford, UK: Oxford University Press, 2008), 202.
23. Bureau of Labor Statistics. "American Time Use Survey." 2004-2008m www,bls.gov/tus/.
24. Jackson, *Distracted*.
25. Carr, *The Shallows*.
26. Ibid, 55.
27. Jackson, *Distracted*.
28. Healy, *Failure to Connect*.
29. J. Rouet, & J. Levonen, "Studying and Learning with Hypertext: Empirical Studies and Their Implications," in *Hypertext and Cognition,* ed. J. Rouet, J. Jarmo, A. Dillon, & R. Spiro (Mahway: Erlbaum, 1996), 16-20.
30. D. Niederhauser, R. Reynolds, D. Salmen, & P. Skalmoski, "The Influence of Cognitive Load on Learning from Hypertext," *Journal of Educational Computing Research* 23, no. 3 (2000): 237-55.
31. D. DeStefano & J. LeFevre, "Cognitive Load in Hypertext Reading: A Review," *Computer in Human Behavior* 23, no. 3 (2007): 1616-41.
32. Carr, *The Shallows*.
33. Healy, *Failure to Connect*.
34. M. Richtel, "A Silicon-valley School That Doesn't Compute," *The New York Times,* 2011, A1.

Chapter Five
No Censorship Left Behind
"See No Evil, Hear No Evil, Speak No Evil"

1. George Orwell, *Nineteen Eighty-four* (London, UK: Penguin Books, Ltd, 2004).
2. Nien Chong, *Life and Death in Shanghai* (New York: Penguin Books USA, Inc., 1987).

3. H. Beard and C. Cerf, *The Official Politically Correct Dictionary and Handbook* (New York: Harper Collins, 1992).

4. Diane Ravitch, *The Language Police* (New York: Vintage Books, 2003), 3.

5. Ibid.

6. Ibid.

7. L. Burress, *Battle of the Books: Literary Censorship in the Public Schools, (1950-1985)* (New York: Scarecrow Press, 1989), 74-75.

8. Ravitch, *The Language Police.*

9. Ibid.

10. Ibid, 141.

11. Stephanie Simon, "Texas Textbooks Tout Christian Heritage," http://politi.co/1wgo6XM4. (accessed Sept. 10, 2014).

12. Ibid.

13. Denisa Superville, "Amid Backlash, Colorado Board Rethinks U.S. History Review," *Education Week,* 2014.

14. Ibid.

15. Ravitch, *The Language Police,* 164.

16. Newton, S., "Can Teachers Criticize Creationism in the Classroom," *Huffingtonpost.com.* (accessed Aug. 30, 2011), 1.

17. G. Lukanoff & J. Haidt, "The Coddling of the American Mind," http://www.theatlantic.com/magazine/archive/2015/09/the-coddling-of-the-american-mind/399356/

18. Ibid.

19. Jenny Jarvie, "Trigger Happy," https://newrepublic.com/article/116842/trigger-warnings-have-spread-blogs-college-classes-thats-bad

20. Newton, S., "Can Teachers Criticize Creationism in the Classroom," *Huffingtonpost.com.* (accessed Aug. 30, 2011), 1.

21. Mark Twain, *The Adventures of Huckleberry Finn* (New York: Bantam Dell, 2003), 85-86.

22. James Hurst, *The Collection of Wonder, (creative short stories)* (Grand Blanc: Creative Education, 1998).

23. Ibid.

Chapter Six
No Child Left Behind
"Policy Plumbers to the Rescue"

1. Ken Kesey, *One Flew Over the Cuckoo's Nest* (New York: The Viking Press, 1962).

2. Philip K. Howard, *The Death of Common Sense: How Law is Suffocating America* (New York: Random House Publishing, 1994), 135-137.

3. Diane Ravitch, *The Death and Life of the Great American School System* (New York: Basic Books, 2010).

4. R. Stake, "Differentiation and Standardization of Aims," *American Educational Research Association* (1993): 3-10.

5. L. Anderson, "The No Child Left Behind Act and the Legacy of Federal aid to Education," *Education Policy Analysis Archives* 13, no. 24 (2005): 1-20.

6. P. Pederson, "What is Measured is Treasured: The Impact of the No Child Left Behind Act on Non-assessed Subjects" *Clearing House* 80, no. 6 (2007): 287-291.

7. D. Orlich, "No Child Left Behind: An Illogical Accountability Model," *Clearing House* 78, no. 1(2004): 6-10.

8. Ibid.

9. Ibid.

10. H. Mintrop and G. Sunderman, "Predictable Failure of Federal Sanctions-driven Accountability for School Improvement and Why We May Retain It Anyway," *American Educational Research Association* 38 (2009): 353-364.

11. Ravitch, *The Death and Life of the Great American School System*.

12. Ibid.

13. Ibid.

14. R. Linn, "The Concept of Validity in the Context of NCLB," in *The Concept of Validity: Revisions, New Directions, and Applications*, ed. Robert W. Lissitz (Charlotte: Information Age Publishing, 2009), 195-212.

15. D. Orlich, "No Child Left Behind: An Illogical Accountability Model," *Clearing House* 78, no. 1(2004): 6-10.

16. L. Guisbond and M. Neill, "Failing Our Children: No Child Left Behind Undermines Quality and Equity in Education," *Clearing House* 78, no. 1 (2004): 12-16.

17. Ravitch, *The Death and Life of the Great American School System*.

18. C. Finn, Jr. and M. Petrilli, Forward to *The Proficiency Illusion*, by John Cronin et al. (Washington D.C.: Thomas B. Fordham Institute and Northwest Evaluation Association, 2007), 3.

19. Orlich, "No Child Left Behind: An Illogical Accountability Model," 6-10.

20. Ibid.

21. Ibid.

22. Ravitch, *The Death and Life of the Great American School System*.

23. Ibid.

24. D. Meier & G. Wood, eds., *Many Children Left Behind: How the No Child Left Behind Act is Damaging Our Children and Our Schools* (Boston: Beacon Press, 2004).

25. Ibid.

26. Ravitch, *The Death and Life of the Great American School System*.

27. D. Meier & G. Wood, eds., *Many Children Left Behind*.

28. Orlich, "No Child Left Behind: An Illogical Accountability Model," 6-10.

29. Constitution of the United States of America. *Fifth Amendment*.

30. B. Starnes, "NCLB Heads Down Alice's Rabbit Hole," *Educational Digest* 70, no. 8 (2005):1-3.

31. E. Correa, "Pedagogy of the Obsessed : Shifting the Focus," *College Quarterly* 9, no. 3 (2006): 1-6.

32. Education Nation, msnbc.com

33. Guisbond and Neill, "Failing Our Children: No Child Left Behind Undermines Quality and Equity in Education,"12-16.

34. Ibid.

35. David Elkind, *The Hurried Child* (Cambridge: Perseus Publishing, 2002).

36. L. Mabry & J. Margolis, "NCLB: Local Implementation and Impact in Southwest Washington State," *Education Policy Analysis Archives* 14, no. 23 (2006).

37. Elkind, *The Hurried Child*.

38. S. Mathison, "The Accumulation of Disadvantage: The Role of Educational Testing in the School Career of Minority Children," *Workplace* 5, no. 2 (2003), 323.

39. Elkind, *The Hurried Child*.

40. R. Pittella, *How Deconstructing the American School System will Reconstruct the American Dream* (Genside: The One Voice Institute of Elemental Ethics and Education, 2011), 61.

41. Ibid, 193.

42. Duncan, A. (2011). Race to the Top Program Description. Ed.gov. *U.S. Department of Education*.

43. Office of the Press Secretary. (2009). Fact Sheet: The Race to the Top. The White House.

44. "Rat Race," DVD, directed by Jerry Zucker (Paramount Pictures, 2001).

45. Pittella, *How Deconstructing the American School System will Reconstruct the American Dream*.

46. Summary of the Every Student Succeeds Act, Legislation, Reauthorizing the Elementary and Secondary Education Act. http://www.ncsl.org/documents/capitolforum/2015/onlineres ources/summary 12 10.pdf

47. "Zen Inspirations: Empty Your Cup,"
www.mindfueldaily.com/livewell/inspirations-from-zen-story-
empty-your-cup#sthash.jcrQbUIA.dpuf.

48. Krishnamurti, *Think on These Things* (New York: Harper and
Row, Publishers, Inc., 1964).

Chapter Seven
No Corporation Left Behind
"The Customer is Always Right"

1. Common Dreams, "Occupy Wall Street Marks One Month at
Liberty Square: Occupations Spread to Over 100 Cities,"
www.commondream.org. (accessed Oct. 17, 2011), 1.

2. Gary Cross, *Kids' Stuff: Toys and the Changing World of American
Childhood* (Cambridge: Harvard University Press, 1999).

3. Ibid, 32.

4. Henry Giroux, *Stealing Innocence: Corporate Culture's War on
Children* (New York: Palgrave Publishing, Ltd, 2000).

5. D. Kunkel, "Children and Television Advertising," *Handbook of
Children and Media,* eds. Dorothy G. Singer & Jerome L. Singer
(Thousand Oaks: Sage Publication, 2001), 375-393.

6. Giroux, *Stealing Innocence,* 15.

7. Deron Boyles, ed., *Schools or Markets: Commercialism, Privatization,
and School-business Partnership* (Mahwah: Lawrence Erlbaum
Associates, Inc., 2005), 70.

8. Morris Berman, *Dark Ages America: The Final Phase of Empire*
(New York: W.W. Norton & Company, Inc., 2006), 33.

9. Ibid.

10. Boyles, ed. *Schools or Markets,* 1.

11. Ibid, 47.

12. Ibid, 47.

13. Ibid, 47.

14. "2011 Summit Conference New York, NY,"
www.educationnation.org., (2011).

15. Giroux, *Stealing Innocence.*

16. Eric Schlosser, *Fast Food Nation: The Dark Side of the All American
Meal* (New York: Perennial, 2002), 51.

17. Boyles, ed. *Schools or Markets.*

18. Ibid.

19. P. Anderson & K. Butcher, K., *"Reading, Writing, and Raisinets:
Are School Finances Contributing to Children's Obesity?"* National
Bureau of Economic Research Paper No. 11177. (2005).

20. N. Wiles et al., "Junk Food, Diet and Childhood Behavioural Problems: Results from the Alspac Cohort," *European Journal of Clinical Nutrition* (2009).
21. Schlosser, *Fast Food Nation.*
22. Anderson, P. & Butcher, K. *"Reading, Writing, and Raisinets: Are School Finances Contributing to Children's Obesity?"*
23. Ibid.
24. Children Now Conference, *"The Future of Children's Media: Advertising Conference,"* New York, NY. (2006).
25. Boyles, ed. *Schools or Markets,* 11.
26. D. Eschmeyer, "House Passes Resolution Promoting Farm to School Programs," *www.FarmtoSchool.org.* (accessed Nov. 19, 2010).
27. Ibid.
28. Jamie Oliver, "Jamie Oliver's Food Revolution." www.WatchJamieOliver.com. (accessed June 3, 2010).
29. R. Greenwald, "There Are Many More Koch Brother Secret Sins," *www.truth-out.org/there-are-many-more-koch-brother-secret-sins/1317648865.* (accessed Oct. 8, 2011).
30. Stephanie Simon, "Koch Group, Unions Battle Over Colorado Schools' Race," www.politico.com. (accessed Nov 2, 2013).
31. Ibid.
32. Ibid.
33. Koch Brothers Exposed, dir. Robert Greenwald, Brave New Foundations, 2012.
34. Boyles, ed. *Schools or Markets.*
35. Ibid.
36. Eric Fromm, *To Have or To Be* (New York: Continuum, 1976).
37. Boyles, ed. *Schools or Markets,* 62.
38. Ibid, 63.
39. Doris Lessing, *The Golden Notebook* (New York: Bantam Books published by arrangement with Simon and Schuster, Inc., 1973), xv-xvii.
40. Boyles, ed. *Schools or Markets.*
41. M. Scott Peck, *The Road Less Travelled: A New Psychology of Love, Traditional Values, and Spiritual Growth* (New York: Touchstone, 2003).
42. W. Mischel et al., "Willpower Over the Life Span: Decomposing Self-regulation," *Social Cognitive and Affective Neuroscience* 6, no. 2 (2011): 252-256.
43. H. Wokusch, "Leaving Wisdom Behind: Corporate Mentality Seizes National Consciousness,"

(www.heatherwokusch.com/index.php?name=News&file=artic
le&sid=21.) (accessed Mar. 14, 2009).

44. R. Archibold, "Applying Corporate Touch to a Troubled
    School District," *The New York Times,* 1999, A28.

45. Giroux, *Stealing Innocence.*

46. Diane Ravitch, *The Death and Life of the Great American School
    System* (New York: Basic Books, 2010).

47. Ibid.

48. Ibid.

49. Ibid.

50. Ibid, 61.

51. Stanley, J., "School House Rocked," *Colorado Springs Independent,*
    2010.

52. Ibid.

53. Ibid.

54. Ibid.

55. McGraw, C., "Sierra Students Protest, Then Take Concerns to
    Board Meeting, *The Gazette,* 2011.

56. Anonymous, KKTV.COM blog posting (2011).

57. Ravitch, *The Death and Life of the Great American School System.*

58. C. Sylvia, "The Corporate Hijacking of Public Education,"
    www.Truth-out.org. (accessed Apr. 16, 2011).

59. Ibid.

60. Ibid.

61. L. Clawson, "Education Data Matters When It Can Be Used
    Against Teachers, but Michelle Rhee Retains Teflon Coat.
    www.dailykos.com. (accessed Feb. 28, 2012).

62. Ibid.

63. Resmovits, J., "Michelle Rhee will Leave CEO Job at
    Studentsfirst, Group She Founded," *Huffington Post,* 2014.

64. Ibid.

65. C. Hedges, "Why the United States is Destroying Its Education
    System,"
    *www.truthdig.com/report/item/why_the_united_states_is_destroying_its_
    educationsystem_20110410/.* (accessed Apr. 11, 2011).

66. J. Hing, "The Eucation of Jose Pedraza: Why Fixing Schools
    Isn't Simple Math," *www.Truth-out.org.* (accessed May 11, 2011).

67. J. Faulk, "Seeking Talented Trainers!" *Teacher Presenters
    Wanted>seekingtalentededucators@faulkjoanna.bmsend.com> on behalf
    of Teacher Presenters Wanted >seekingtalentededucators@gmail.com>*
    (2012).

68. William Deresiewicz, *Excellent Sheep: The Miseducation of the
    American Elite and the Way to a Meaningful Life* (New York: Free

Press, 2014), 174.

69. Ravitch, *The Death and Life of the Great American School System.*
70. Boyles, ed. *Schools or Markets.*
71. Diane Ravitch, *Reign of Error: The Hoax of the Privatization Movement and the Danger to America's Public Schools* (New York: Alfred A. Knopf, 2013), 19-20.
72. Ravitch, *The Death and Life of the Great American School System.*
73. Ibid.
74. Henry Giroux, *Education and the Crisis of Public Values (Counterpoints: Studies in Postmodern Theory of Education)* (New York: Peter Lang Publishing, 2011), 18.
75. "Waiting for Superman, DVD, directed by David Guggenheim (Walden Media, 2010).
76. Ibid.
77. Ravitch, *Reign of Error,* 168.
78. Ibid., 172.
79. B. Herold, "Virtual Blended Schools Growing Despite Struggles, Analysis Finds." http://blogs.edweek.org/edweek/DigitalEducation/2016/04/virtual_blended_schools_NEPC.html?qs=math (accessed May 20, 2016).
80. Ibid.
81. V. Strauss, "Education Activists Seek to Collaborate with Occupy Wall Street," *The Answer Sheet: A School Survival Guide for Parents (And Everyone Else)* (2011):2-5.

Chapter Eight
No Conversation Left Behind
"Chalk Talk"

1. Smith, S., "No Foolin': Old-school New School," *Pueblo Chieftain Newspaper,* 2012.
2. Ibid.
3. B. O'Reilly, "The O'Reilly Factor," *www.billoreilly.com.* (2012).
4. Pasi Sahlberg, *Finnish Lessons: What can the World Learn from Educational Change in Finland?* (New York: Teachers College Press, 2011), xv.
5. Eric Thompson, "What is 21st Century Learning?" *www.ehow.com.* (accessed Sept. 18, 2012).
6. Ibid.
7. E. Silva, "Measuring Skills for the 21st Century," *www.educationsector.org.* (accessed Nov. 3, 2008).

8. Partnership for 21st Century Skills, "Framework for 21st Century Learning," *www.P21.org*. (accessed May 6, 2009).
9. Ibid.
10. Erik Erikson, *Childhood and Society* (New York: W.W. Norton and Company, 1993).
11. Ibid.
12. Sahlberg, *Finnish Lessons*.
13. Ibid.
14. A. Partanen, "What Americans Keep Ignoring about Finland's School Success," *www.theatlantic.com/national/print/2011/12/what-americans-keep-ignoring-about-f...* (accessed Dec. 29, 2011).

Chapter Nine
No Creativity Left Behind
"Putting the FUN Back into DysFUNction"

1. A. Ishaq, "On the Importance of Creativity: Fostering Creativity in Children Through Arts. *www.icaf.org*. (accessed Jan. 5, 2014).
2. S. Kerka, "Creativity in Adulthood," *ERIC Digest* No. 204 (1999): 1-7.
3. Mihaly Csikszentmihalyi, *Creativity: Flow and the Psychology of Discovery and Invention* (New York: HarperCollins Publishers, Inc., 1996).
4. Ibid.
5. M. Anderson, "Play," *www.deltaskymag.com*. (2011).
6. Ken Robinson, "Do Schools Kill Creativity?" www.ted.com. (accessed June 18, 2010).
7. J. Jacobson & P. Phillips, "Creativity in the Workplace," *Academy of Management Journal* 39, no. 5 (2007):1154.
8. R. Upitis, K. Smithrim, J. Garbati, H. Ogden, "The Impact of Art-making in the University Workplace," *International Journal of Education and the Arts* 9, no. 8 (2008): 2-24.
9. P. Stanistreet, "A Virtually Limitless Resource," *Adults Learning* (2008): 12-15.
10. A. Partanen, "What Americans Keep Ignoring about Finland's School Success," *www.theatlantic.com/national/print/2011/12/what-americans-keep-ignoring-about-f...* (accessed Dec. 29, 2011).
11. Ken Robinson, *The Element* (New York: Penguin Group, 2009), 259.
12. Julia Cameron, *The Artist's Way: A Spiritual Path to Higher Creativity* (New York: Penguin Putnam, Inc., 1992).

13. Erik Erikson, *Childhood and Society* (New York: W.W. Norton and Company, 1993).

Chapter Ten
Leaving My Classroom Behind
"A Teary Tale"

1. "Julia," DVD, directed by Fred Zinnemann (20th Century Fox, 1977).
2. L. P. Hartley, *The Go Between* (New York: New York Review Books, 1953), 1.

Bibliography

1. Adams, James Truslow. *The Epic of America.* Piscataway: Transaction Publishers, 2012.
2. Abbott, J., P. Leith, & H. MacTaggart. *Over-schooled but Undereducated: How the Crisis in Education is Jeopardizing Our Adolescents.* New York: Continuum International Publishing Group, 2010.
3. Anderson, L. "The No Child Left Behind Act and the Legacy of Federal Aid to Education." *Education Policy Analysis Archives*, 13, no. 24 (2005): 1-20.
4. Anderson, M. "Play." www.deltaskymag.com. (accessed 2011).
5. Anderson, P. & K. Butcher. "Reading, Writing, and Raisinets: Are School Finances Contributing to Children's Obesity?" *National Bureau of Economic Research Paper No. 11177,* 2005.
6. Anonymous, (2011). KKTV.COM blog posting.
7. Archibold, R. "Applying Corporate Touch to a Troubled School District." *The New York Times,* 1999, A28.
8. Baron, N. *Always On: Language in an Online and Mobile World.* Oxford: Oxford University Press, 2008.
9. Batton, J. "The 'New Narcissism' in 20th Century America: The Shadow and Substance of Social Change." *Journal of Social History* 17, no. 2 (1983): 199-220.
10. Bauerlein, M. *The Dumbest Generation: How the Digital Age Stupefies Young Americans and Jeopardizes Our Future.* New York: W.W. Norton and Company, Inc., 2008.
11. Beard, H. and C. Cerf. *The Official Politically Correct Dictionary and Handbook.* New York: Harper Collins, 1992.
12. Becker, Ernest. *The Denial of Death.* New York: Free Press Paperbacks, 1973.
13. Being There. dir. Hal Ashby, perf. Peter Sellers, DVD, Warner Bros., 1979.
14. Bell, James. "China Seen Overtaking U.S. as Global Superpower." *PEW Global Attitudes Project,* July 13, 2011.
15. Berman, M. *Dark Ages America: The Final Phase of Empire.* New York: W.W. Norton & Company, Inc., 2006.
16. Boyles, Deron, ed. *School s or Markets: Commercialism, Privatization, and School-business Partnerships.* Mahwah. Lawrence Erlbaum Associates, Inc., 2005.

17. Bradbury, R. *The Illustrated Man*. New York: Simon and Schuster, 2012.
18. Bureau of Labor Statistics. "American Time Use Survey." 2004-2008m www.bls.gov/tus/.
19. Burress, L. *Battle of the Books: Literary Censorship in the Public Schools, (1950-1985*. New York: Scarecrow Press, 1989.
20. Cameron, Julia. *The Artist's Way: A Spiritual Path to Higher Creativity*. New York: Penguin Putnam, Inc., 1992.
21. Campbell, Joseph. *The Power of Myth*. New York: Anchor Books, 1988.
22. Carr, N. *The Shallows: What the Internet is Doing to Our Brains*. New York: W.W. Norton & Company, Inc., 2010.
23. Chong, N. *Life and Death in Shanghai*. New York: Penguin Books USA, Inc., 1987.
24. Children Now Conference. *The Future of Children's Media: Advertising Conference*, 2006. New York, NY.
25. Cobb, Ron. *The Cobb Book: Cartoons*. Sydney, Australia: Wild and Woolley Press, 1975.
26. Constitution of the United States of America. *Fifth Amendment*.
27. Correa, E. "Pedagogy of the Obsessed Shifting the Focus." *College Quarterly* 9, no. 3 (2006): 1-6.
28. Cross, G. *Kids' Stuff: Toys and the Changing World of American Childhood*. Cambridge: Harvard University Press, 1999.
29. Clawson, L. "Education Data Matters When It can be Used Against Teachers, but Michelle Rhee Retains Teflon Coat." *www.dailykos.com*. (accessed Feb. 28, 2012).
30. Csikszentmihalyi, M. *Creativity: Flow and the Psychology of Discovery and Invention*. New York: Harper Collins Publishers, Inc., 1996.
31. Csikszentmihalyi, M. *Finding Flow: The Psychology of Engagement with Everyday Life*. New York: Basic Books, 1997.
32. Declaration of Independence.
33. Deresiewicz, W. *Excellent Sheep: The Miseducation of the American Elite and the Way to a Meaningful Life*. New York: Free Press, 2014.
34. DeStefano, D. & J. LeFevre. "Cognitive Load in Hypertext Reading: A Review." *Computer in Human Behavior*, 23, no. 3 (2007): 1616-41.
35. Dickens, C. *A Tale of Two Cities*. New York: Bantam Classics, 1989.
36. Dr. Shirley Robbins.

37. Duncan, A. Race to the Top Program Description. Ed.gov. *U.S. Department of Education*, 2011.

38. Education Nation, msnbc.com.

39. Elkind, D. *The Hurried Child.* Cambridge: Perseus Publishing, 2002.

40. Erikson, E. *Childhood and Society.* New York: W.W. Norton and Company, 1993.

41. Eschmeyer, D. "House Passes Resolution Promoting Farm to School Programs." *www.FarmtoSchool.org.* (accessed Nov. 19, 2010).

42. Faulk, J. "Seeking Talented Trainers!" *Teacher Presenters Wanted>seekingtalentededucators@faulkjoanna.bmsend.com>on behalf of Teacher Presenters Wanted >seekingtalentededucators@gmail.com>*, 2012.

43. Finn, Jr., C and M. Petrilli. Forward to *The Proficiency Illusion*, by John Cronin et al. (Washington D.C.: Thomas B. Fordham Institute and Northwest Evaluation Association), 2007.

44. Fromm, Eric. *To Have or To Be.* New York: Continuum, 1976.

45. Giroux, H. *Education and the Crisis of Public Values: Challenging the Assault on Teachers, Students, and Public Education.* New York: Peter Lang Publishing, Inc., 2012.

46. Giroux, H. *Stealing Innocence: Corporate Culture's War on Children.* New York: Palgrave Publishing, Ltd., 2000.

47. Goldson, E. "Here I Stand: Valedictorian Speaks Out Against Schooling in Graduation Speech." www.sott.net. (accessed June 25, 2010).

48. Greenberger, E., J. Lessard, C. Chen, & S. Farrugia. "Self-entitled College Students: Contributions of Personality, Parenting, and Motivational Factors." *Journal of Youth, Adolescence,* 2008, no. 37: 1193-1204.

49. Greenwald, R. "There are Many More Koch Brother Secret Sins." *www.truth-out.org/there-are-many-more-koch-brother-secret-sins/1317648865.* (accessed Oct. 8, 2011).

50. Guisbond, L. and M. Neill. "Failing Our Children: No Child Left Behind Undermines Quality and Equity in Education." *Clearing House* 78, no. 1 (2004): 12-16.

51. Healy, J. *Failure to Connect: How Computers Affect Our Children's Minds—and What We Can Do About It.* New York: Simon & Schuster Paperbacks, 1998.

52. Hedges, C. "Why the United States is Destroying Its Education System."
_www.truthdig.com/report/item/why_the_united_states_is_destroying_its_education_system_20110410/_ (accessed Apr. 11, 2011).

53. Hendrick, H. "Optimism and Hope Versus Anxiety and Narcissism: Some Thoughts on Children's Welfare Yesterday and Today." _History of Education_ 37, no. 6 (2007): 747-768.

54. Herold, B. "Virtual, Blended Schools Growing Despite Struggles, Analysis Finds. http://blogs.edweek.org/edweek/DigitalEducation/2016/04/virtual_blended_schools_NEPC.html?qs=math

55. Hing, J. "The Education of Jose Pedraza: Why Fixing Schools isn't Simple Math." _www.Truth-out.org._ (accessed May 11, 2011).

56. Howard, Philip K. _The Death of Common Sense: How Law is Suffocating America._ New York: Random House, Inc., 1994.

57. Hurst, J. _The Collection of Wonder, (Creative Short Stories)._ Grand Blanc. Creative Education, 1998.

58. Ishaq, A. "On the Importance of Creativity: Fostering Creativity in Children Through Arts." _www.icaf.org._ (accessed Jan. 5, 2014).

59. Jarvie, Jenny, "Trigger Happy," https://newrepublic.com/article/116842/trigger-warnings-have-spread-blogs-college-classes-thats-bad

60. Jackson, M. _Distracted: The Erosion of Attention and the Coming Dark Age._ Amherst: Prometheus Books, 2008.

61. Jacobson, J. & P. Phillips. "Creativity in the Workplace." _Academy of Management Journal_ 39, no. 5 (2007): 1154.

62. James, W. _The Principles of Psychology._ Mineola: Dover Publications: reprint edition, 1950.

63. "Julia," DVD, directed by Fred Zinnemann (20th Century Fox, 1977).

64. Hartley, L. P. _The Go Between._ New York: New York Review Books, 1953.

65. Kaiser Family Foundation. "Study Shows Kids Tethered to Technology." http://abcnes.go.com/WN/kids-electronics-study-shows-kids-spend-hours-day/story?id=9... (accessed Jan 20, 2010).

66. Kerka, S. "Creativity in Adulthood." *ERIC Digest,* 1999, no. 204: 1-7.

67. Kernberg, O. *Borderline Conditions and Pathological Narcissism.* Lanham. Rowman and Littlefield Publishers, Inc., 1985.

68. Kesey, K. *One Flew Over the Cuckoo's Nest.* New York: The Viking Press, 1962.

69. Klorer, P. "The Effects of Technological Overload on Children: An Art Therapist's Perspective." *Art Therapy: Journal of the American Art Therapy Association* 26, no. 2 (2009): 80-82.

70. Krishnamurti. *Think on These Things.* New York: Harper and Row, Publishers, Inc., 1964.

71. Koch Brothers Exposed, dir. Robert Greenwald, Brave New Foundations, 2012.

72. Kunkel, D. "Children and Television Advertising." In *Handbook of Children and Media,* edited by Dorothy G. Singer & Jerome L. Singer, 375-393. Thousand Oaks. Sage Publications, 2001.

73. Lasch, Christopher. *The Culture of Narcissism: American Life in a Time of Diminishing Expectations.* New York: W.W. Norton & Company, Inc., 1991.

74. Le Beau, J. "The 'Silver Spoon' Syndrome in the Super Rich: The Pathological Linkage of Affluence and Narcissism in Family Systems." *American journal of psychotherapy* 52, no. 3 (1988): 425-436.

75. Lenhart, A. "Teens, Cell Phones and Texting: Text Messaging Becomes Centerpiece of Communication." *Pew Internet and American Life Project,* 2010.

76. Lessing, D. *The Golden Notebook.* New York. Bantam Books published by arrangement with Simon and Schuster, Inc., 1973.

77. Leunig, M. *The Penguin Leunig.* Camberwell, Australia: Penguin Group, 1974.

78. Linn, R. "The Concept of Validity in the Context of NCLB." In *The Concept of Validity: Revisions, New Directions, and Applications,* edited by Robert W. Lissitz, 195-212. Charlotte. Information Age Publishing, 2009.

79. London, Jack. *The Call of the Wild, White Fang, and to Build a Fire.* New York: Modern Library Classics, 2012.

80. Lukanoff, G. & Haidt, J. "The Coddling of the American Mind," http://www.theatlantic.com/magazine/archive/2015/09/the-coddling-of-the-american-mind/399356/

81. Lum, L. "Handling Helicopter Parents." *Diverse: Issues in Higher Education* 23, no. 20 (2006): 40-43.

82. Mabry, L. & J. Margolis. "NCLB: Local Implementation and Impact in Southwest Washington State." *Education Policy Analysis Archives* 14, no. 23 (2006).

83. Marano, H. *A Nation of Whimps*. New York: Broadway Books, 2008.

84. Mathison, S. "The Accumulation of Disadvantage: The Role of Educational Testing in the School Career of Minority Children." *Workplace* 5, no.2 (2003).

85. McGraw, C. "Sierra Students Protest, Then Take Concerns to Board Meeting." *The Gazette*. 2011.

86. Meier, D. & G. Wood, eds. *Many Children Left Behind: How the No Child Left Behind Act is Damaging Our Children and Our Schools*. Boston: Beacon Press, 2004.

87. Melville, Herman. *Moby Dick*. New York: Oxford University Press, 1998.

88. Minority Report. dir. Steven Spielberg. Perf. Tom Cruise, DVD, Paramount, 2002.

89. Mintrop, H. and G. Sunderman. "Predictable Failure of Federal Sanctions-driven Accountability for School Improvement and Why We may Retain It Anyway. *American Educational Research Association*, 2009, no. 38: 353-364.

90. Mischel, W., A. Berman, M. Casey, B. Gotlib, I. Jonides, J. Kross, E. Teslovich, T. Wilson, N. Zayas, V. Shoda, & Yuichi. "Willpower Over the Life Span: Decomposing Self-regulation." *Social Cognitive and Affective Neuroscience* 6, no. 2 (2011): 252-256.

91. Newton, S. "Can Teachers Criticize Creationism in the Classroom." www.*huffingtonpost.com*. (accessed Aug. 30, 2011).

92. Niederhauser, D., R. Reynolds, D. Salmen, & P. Skalmoski. "The Influence of Cognitive Load on Learning from Hypertext." *Journal of Educational Computing Research* 23, no. 3 (2000): 237-55.

93. Occupy Wall Street. "Occupy Wall Street Marks One Month at Liberty Square: Occupations Spread to Over 100 Cities." *www.commondream.org*. (accessed Oct. 17, 2011).

94. Office of the Press Secretary. *Fact Sheet: The Race to the Top.* 2009, The White House.

95. Oliver, Jamie. "Jamie Oliver's Food Revolution." www.WatchJamieOliver.com. (accessed June 3, 2010).

96. O'Reilly, B. "The O'Reilly Factor." *www.billoreilly.com.* (2012).

97. Orlich, D. "No Child Left Behind: An Illogical Accountability Model." *Clearing House* 78, no. 1 (2004): 6-10.

98. Ornstein, R. *The Evolution of Consciousness: The Origin of the Way We Think.* New York: Simon & Schuster Paperbacks, 1991.

99. Orwell, G. *Nineteen Eighty-four.* London: Penguin Books, Ltd., 2004.

100. Pape, Robert. "Empire Falls." *The National Interest* 9, no. 21 (2009).

101. Partanen, A. "What Americans Keep Ignoring about Finland's School Success." *www.theatlantic.com/national/print/2011/12/what-americans-keep-ignoring-about-f...* (accessed Dec. 29, 2011).

102. Partnership for 21st Century Skills. "Framework for 21st Century Learning." *www.P21.org.* (accessed May 6, 2009).

103. Pascuel-Leone, A., A. Amedi, F. Fregni, & B. Merabet. "The Plastic Human Brain Cortex." *Annual Review of Neuroscience,* 2005, no. 28: 377-401.

104. Peck, M. Scott. *The Road Less Travelled: A New Psychology of Love, Traditional Values, and Spiritual Growth.* New York: Touchstone, 2003.

105. Pederson, P. "What is Measured is Treasured: The Impact of the No Child Left Behind Act on Non-assessed Subjects." *Clearing House* 80, no. 6 (2007): 287-291.

106. Pittella, R. *How Deconstructing the American School System will Reconstruct the American Dream.* Genside: The One Voice Institute of Elemental Ethics and Education, 2011.

107. Rich, M. "American 15-year-olds Lag, Mainly in Math, on International Standardized Tests." *The New York Times,* Dec. 3, 2013.

108. Rolvaag, O.E. *Giants in the Earth.* New York: Harper Perennial Publishers, 1991.

109. Rat Race, dir. Jerry Zucker, perf. Rowan Atkinson, DVD, Paramount Pictures, 2001.

110. Ravitch, D. *The Death and Life of the Great American School System.* New York: Basic Books, 2010.

111. Ravitch, D. *The Language Police.* New York: Vintage Books, 2003.

112. Richtel, M. "A Silicon-valley School That Doesn't Compute." *The New York Times,* Oct. 23, 2011, A1.

113. Resmovits, J. "Michelle Rhee Will Leave CEO Job at Studentsfirst, Group She Founded." *Huffington Post,* 2014.

114. Robinson, K. "Do Schools Kill Creativity?" www.ted.com. (accessed June 18, 2010).

115. Robinson, K. *The Element.* New York: Penguin Group, 2009.

116. Rouet, J. & J. Levonen. "Studying and Learning with Hypertext: Empirical Studies and Their Implications." In *Hypertext and Cognition,* ed. Jean-Francois Rouet, Jarmo J. Levonen, Andrew Dillon, & Rand J. Spiro, 16-20. Mahway. Erlbaum, 1996.

117. Sahlberg, P. *Finnish Lessons: What Can the World Learn from Educational Change in Finland?* New York: Teachers' College Press, 2011.

118. Schlosser, Eric. *Fast Food Nation: The Dark Side of the All American Meal.* New York: Perennial, 2002.

119. Simon, Stephanie, "Koch Brothers, Union Battle Over Colorado School's Race." www.politico.com/story/2013/11/koch-group- unions-battle...(accessed Nov. 2, 2013).

120. Simon, Stephanie, "Texas Textbooks Tout Christian Heritage." http://politi.co/1wgo6XM4. (accessed Sept. 10, 2014).

121. Silva, E. "Measuring Skills for the 21st Century." *www.educationsector.org* (accessed Nov. 3, 2008).

122. Smith, S. "No Foolin': Old-school New School." *Pueblo Chieftain,* 2012.

123. Stake, R. "Differentiation and Standardization of Aims." *American Educational Research Association,* 1993, 3-10.

124. Starnes, B. "NCLB Heads Down Alice's Rabbit Hole." *Educational Digest* 70, no. 8 (2005): 1-3.

125. Stanistreet, P. "A Virtually Limitless Resource." *Adults Learning* 20, no.4 (2008): 12-15.

126. Stanley, J. (2010). "School House Rocked." *Colorado Springs Independent,* 2010, 17-21.

127. Strauss, V. "Education Activists Seek to Collaborate With

Occupy Wall Street." *The Answer Sheet: A School Survival Guide for Parents (And Everyone Else)*, 2011, 2-5.

128. Summary of the Every Student Succeeds Act, Legislation, Reauthorizing the Elementary and Secondary Education Act. http://www.ncsl.org/documents/capitolforum/2015/onlines ources/summary/1210.pdf.

129. Superville, Denisa, "Amid Backlash, Colorado Board Rethinks U.S. History Review," *Education Week*, 2014.

130. Sylvia, C. "The Corporate Hijacking of Public Education. www.Truth- out.org. (accessed April 16, 2011).

131. The Finland Phenomenon: Inside the World's Most Surprising School System. dir. Sean Faust. perf. Tony Wagner, DVD, True South Studios, 2011.

132. Thompson, Eric. "What is 21st Century Learning?" www.ehow.com. (accessed Sept. 18, 2012).

133. Thomson, I. "The Theory That Won't Die: From Mass Society to the Decline of Social Capital." *Sociological Forum* 20, no. 3 (2005): 421-448.

134. Twain, M. *The Adventures of Huckleberry Finn*. New York. Bantam Dell, 2003.

135. Twenge, J., and W. Campbell. *The Narcissism Epidemic*. New York: Free Press, 2009.

136. Tyler, Imogen. "The Me Decade' to the Me Millennium': The Cultural History of Narcissism." *International Journal of Cultural Studies*, 2007, no.10: 343.

137. Upitis, R., K. Smithrim, J. Garbati, H. Ogden. "The Impact of Art making in the University Workplace." *International Journal of Education and the Arts* 9, no. 8 (2008): 2-24.

138. Wiles, N. "Junk Food, Diet and Childhood Behavioural Problems: Results from the Alspac Cohort." *European Journal of Clinical Nutrition*, 2009.

139. Wills, E. "Parent Trap." *The Chronicle of Higher Education 5*, no. 46 (2005): 1-2.

140. Wokusch, H. "Leaving Wisdom Behind: Corporate Mentality Seizes National Consciousness." www.heatherwokusch.com/index.php?name=News&file=articl e&sid=21. (accessed Mar. 14, 2009).

141. Summit Conference. New York, NY. www.educationnation.org. (accessed 2011).

142. Young-Eisendreth, P. *The Self-esteem Trap*. Boston: Little Brown and Company, 2005.

Acknowledgments

I would like to thank Douglas Tureck for inspiring me to become a teacher, for encouraging me to write "Taking Back Our Classrooms," and for his masterful initial editing of the book. Thank you to my sister Patty Brudeseth for her skillful final editing of the book and for her encouragement and to Rick Brudeseth for his astute suggestions. Thank you also to Dominic Race for his recommendations and to Andrea Emmett for her continual supply of newspaper articles about American education. A final thanks goes to members of my writing group—Patty Brudeseth, Susan Conley, and Shirley Robbins—for their support throughout the writing process

About Barbara

Barbara spent 38 years in the classroom, both in Australia and the United States. She taught language arts, literature, speech, drama, theater studies, media studies, history, and alternative life styles to students from 5th to 12th grade in public, private, and culturally diverse schools in inner city, suburban, and country settings.

She has a BS in English and history with a minor in political science; a post-graduate degree in drama in education; a post-graduate degree in media studies; and a master's degree in adult education and training with a focus on creativity in education. She has also done coursework in environmental science, educational counseling, and arts' management.

She has travelled the world and is an avid reader of fiction, history, politics, philosophy, sociology, psychology, and current affairs.

Contact Information

barbdrama@yahoo.com
www.takingbackourclassrooms.com
"Drama Unmasked" store on www.teacherspayteachers.com
www.facebook.com: Taking Back Our Classrooms
Also available from www.amazon.com, www.CreateSpace.com,
and other retail outlets

Books can be ordered directly from Barbara at her email address:
barbdrama@yahoo.com

www.ingramcontent.com/pod-product-compliance
Lightning Source LLC
LaVergne TN
LVHW021449080426
835509LV00018B/2214